Boundary Crossers:
Community Leadership for a Global Age

Neal Peirce & Curtis Johnson
Foreword by John W. Gardner

John W. Gardner
Georgia Sorenson
Co-Chairs
Citizen Participation & Political Leadership Focus Group
Kellogg Leadership Studies Project

Bruce Adams
John Parr
Project Directors

Curtis Johnson
Harold McDougall
Suzanne Morse
Neal Peirce
Annette Rogers
Robert Rosen

With Support Provided by
Ewing Marion Kauffman Foundation
W.K. Kellogg Foundation

A Project of the
The James MacGregor Burns Academy of Leadership
University of Maryland

The Burns Academy of Leadership Press

"This pioneering report by Neal Peirce and Curtis Johnson gives a vivid sense of what is happening in metropolitan America and provides hope for the future of our communities. The Peirce-Johnson report is a valuable learning tool for community builders designed to help sharpen the skills of citizen leaders in every sector. Peirce and Johnson draw from their extensive knowledge of the cities of this country, as well as from the in-depth case studies compiled for this project, to give us ten important lessons for community builders and to suggest ways to develop new strategies for dealing with the challenges that face our communities."

— John W. Gardner

CONTENTS

Boundary Crossers:
Community Leadership for a Global Age

Success in cities is often heralded as a story of civic perseverance in the face of extreme crisis. After Cleveland became a national embarrassment, its leadership finally realized the depth of the problem, picked up the pieces and rebuilt the city. In Denver, when the energy companies that led the boom busted in the 1980s, that crisis forced leaders to forge a balanced economy. But a lack of crisis can be dangerous. San Diego has all the exterior signs of health, but complacency has led to serious unattended problems. The lessons of Portland and Charlotte prove, though, that even in the absence of civic meltdown, smart cities can solve problems before they loom large.

Hard as the nails and mortar revitalization of some inner cities has been, the shiny new buildings and newly-bustling downtowns are the easy part. The more difficult question is how to improve the lives of those still caught in dead-end ghettos of poverty and hopelessness. Progress is possible: in Chattanooga, concerted, intensive efforts have led to turnarounds. But the vast majority of cities face huge questions: How can areas outside the inner cities be convinced to take responsibility for the poor concentrated inside? How can people of different races and backgrounds get along well enough to solve problems together? People are talking about the problems and possible answers. That isn't a solution, but it is a powerful first step.

The message from a wide variety of cities in the United States is that there is no all-purpose governance structure that works today. What matters instead is organizing governance based on a community's strengths — and recognizing that it is the relationships among people that get things done. In Cleveland, business takes the lead. In Denver, government and business have a successful partnership. San Antonio's governance style is prodded by citizen organizations. In every case of successful leadership, it is not the structure that matters, but the way people work together to get things done.

Everyone has to chip in to make the mix work. Universities, professions, faith communities, and the media are top among the candidates to enrich the leadership mix. The University of California at San Diego spawned the San Diego Dialogue to get tough issues on the regional agenda. In Cleveland, a farsighted bishop is mobilizing Catholics to deal with urban sprawl, citing a moral dimension to the isolation of the inner city poor. The *Charlotte Observer* strives for coverage that provides a context for solving community problems.

Charismatic individual leaders can still make things happen. In Charlotte, Nations-Bank Chairman Hugh McColl convinced his company to buy up devastated city blocks and develop them. In Oregon, legislators, governors, and mayors have spearheaded many successful efforts — from the land use laws to light rail — that have helped shape a lively downtown as the center of a region with a high quality of life. The lesson here is to respect and welcome civic-minded leaders who can make a difference.

Regardless of whether traditional leaders like it, collaboration is here to stay. Once people know they can have a voice, they demand it. The partnerships take many forms. One example is Denver, where governments and businesses joined forces in the 1980s to launch an economic turnaround that continues today. But power-sharing is always difficult, and some learn the language so they can abuse the process. Today, cities are fumbling toward collaboration, making mistakes, and beginning to form new, inclusive institutions that can solve problems.

Most Americans say they don't like their governments, but real change depends on good government. Government's perceived role runs the gamut across the country, from innovator and catalyst in Detroit to leader in Portland. These days, government has a new role — as a bridge between community organizations and business. In all its myriad forms, though, and despite its inefficiencies and problems, we still need government as a partner for real, long term change.

Connect to the Internet all you want — but realize that home counts. The places that matter most today are regions, formed by suburbs and inner cities with a nod to their mutual self-interest despite their mutual antagonism; neighborhoods, increasingly organized and involved in partnerships; and center cities, the heart and soul of every region. Nowhere is the importance of the center city better illustrated than in Portland, where neighborhood-rooted citizen outcry against thoughtless development sparked the creation of a glorious downtown.

Keep your eye on the ball. Los Angeles didn't after the roaring success of the 1984 Olympics, and one result was the shattering riots of 1992. Atlanta is trying to learn from Los Angeles' mistake. No success is ever final. In some cities, one victory leads the drive to another: Chattanooga, which began by improving air quality and reclaiming a river, is now making sustainability the key to its revitalization. In Cleveland, the Rock and Roll Hall of Fame is open and reformers are turning to improving poor schools. In short, no community, however successful, can ever rest on its laurels — or even its lovely waterfront park.

Relationship building across traditional barriers is by definition an unnatural act. It has to be learned. It requires constant, hard work. The co-project directors offer a tool for community builders, a checklist for relationship building and collaborative problem-solving. Also, they recommend a reading list for community builders and boundary crossers and offer their thanks for all who made this work possible.

A note to readers: Unless otherwise stated, in this report the name of a city refers to its entire metropolitan area.

Foreword by John W. Gardner

Reading the morning paper or watching the nightly news, you might think that nothing works anymore. You might conclude that nobody cares much and few are even trying to make a difference.

But you'd be wrong. Dead wrong. There are new signs of vitality all across America. There are many able people working hard for the public good in every community in this nation. And in some places, there are enough of these people to have reached a critical mass and changed the political culture of their communities.

At the time of the fierce urban riots of the late 1960s, the cities were the subject of intense national interest and attention. But when the riots ended, the interest died and was followed by two decades of neglect. Then, a few years ago, new signs of life began to appear. Cities in many parts of the country showed an inclination to take command of their own fate — Charlotte, Chattanooga, Cleveland, Portland and others. There began a wave of innovation in dealing with urban problems — a wave that is continuing in full force.

While theorists debate the virtues of devolution, the dispersion of initiative and responsibility downward and outward through our federal-state-local system, the cities are making it happen.

We are not among the "sentimental localists" who would love to turn their backs on all but the local level. But we cannot flourish nationally or globally if our local communities — the places where our children learn responsibility, where the bonding and accommodation of group functioning are generated — become anarchic environments breeding a rootless and irresponsible people.

Today, in one community after another, the diverse segments and sectors of the community are working together in new patterns of collaboration and partnership. Such patterns don't spring full-blown from the minds of urban planners. They involve much groping, much trial-and-error. We are in a transition to a new way of doing the public's business, but we aren't there yet. Faced with this somewhat tumultuous, shifting scene, some of us decided to have a look at how these developments are actually working in ten important metropolitan areas of the country. A reality check.

Today, in one community after another, the diverse segments and sectors of the community are working together in new patterns of collaboration and partnership.

We didn't try to pick "the ten best cities." We chose lively ones, ones that seem to be moving in the right direction. We chose a cross section of our nation's communities — looking for diversity in geography, demographics, and economics. The metropolitan areas range from Portland, Oregon — on everyone's list of doing it right — to the comeback cities of Chattanooga and Cleveland, and to Detroit, where we see signs of positive change.

This pioneering report by Neal Peirce and Curtis Johnson gives a vivid sense of what is happening in metropolitan America and provides hope for the future of our communities. The Peirce-Johnson report is a valuable learning tool for community builders designed to help sharpen the skills of citizen leaders in every sector. Peirce and Johnson draw from their extensive knowledge of the cities of this country, as well as from the in-depth case studies compiled for this project, to give us ten important lessons for community builders and to suggest ways to develop new strategies for dealing with the challenges that face our communities.

The key is to get people talking and working together across the boundary lines that traditionally divide and diminish a community — people from government, corporations, social agencies, ethnic groups, unions, neighborhoods and so on. These people have usually had little experience in talking with one another, much less collaborating. We found that building healthy communities is less about structure and more about building relationships. Relationship building is the key to breaking political gridlock and being able to take action in the public interest.

There is much left to do. The shortcomings of even these relatively lively cities are evident. None of these communities has dealt effectively with the growing disparity in this country between the haves and have-nots. Nor have they dealt adequately with race. One topic to which Peirce and Johnson give particular attention is the all-important relationship of the city to its region. It is still one of the most neglected aspects of our urban scene. Few cities and suburbs are even willing to think about it, much less take constructive action.

No community can claim to have all the answers. There isn't any model that can be taken off the shelf and installed in your local community. Every community has to find its own solutions and to make them work in its unique circumstances. But the leadership lesson is clear. The citizen leadership we need for the 21st century requires a lot of people from every sector working very hard together to make our communities better places to live, work, and raise our children.

We need to do a better job of recruiting and preparing community builders, from youth to business leaders, to be effective in this new culture of collaboration. We must take special pains to see that people are not left without a voice at the decision-making table because they lack resources.

What we need, and what seems to be emerging in some of our communities, is something new — networks of responsibility drawn from all segments coming together to create a wholeness that incorporates diversity. The participants must come to be at home with change and exhibit a measure of shared values, a sense of mutual obligation and trust. Above all, they must develop a sense of responsibility for the future of the whole city and region.

All of us involved in this venture owe a debt of thanks to Bruce Adams and John Parr for their wise management of this project, to Neal Peirce and Curtis Johnson for an impressive report, and to the Ewing Marion Kauffman Foundation, the W.K. Kellogg Foundation, and The James MacGregor Burns Academy of Leadership at The University of Maryland for sponsoring the project.

What we need, and what seems to be emerging in some of our communities, is something new— networks of responsibility drawn from all segments coming together to create a wholeness that incorporates diversity.

John W. Gardner
Consulting Professor
School of Education
Stanford University
Stanford, California

October 1997

A Civic Vignette: The Chattanooga Story—From Troubled Raw River Town to Global Model

The 1960s and 1970s were hard years for the raw river town of Chattanooga, Tennessee — a town whose ambition had been to be the Pittsburgh of the South, a place of bellowing smokestacks, forging metal, making machinery.

A brown cloud often blanketed the city; cars often had to drive at mid-day with their lights on. Business executives needed two white shirts to get through one day. Many residents remember the day in 1969 that the news came from Washington — Chattanooga had the foulest air of any American city.

A spurt of hope was felt as a local air quality board was created and millions of dollars invested in new technology to combat particulates and nitrous oxides. Yet even as the air began to clear, the Chattanooga industries that had prospered for decades turning out iron castings, nuclear vessels and textiles saw a rapid loss of markets (and jobs) to more modern plants and offshore locations. The city fell into a deep recession.

The 1,700 citizens who took part in Chattanooga Venture, a good social and racial cross-section of the city themselves, were told every idea they wrote down would be seriously considered. An avalanche of ideas was boiled down to 40 truly usable ones.

Racial challenges

Racial trouble struck too. In 1971, simmering differences led to disturbances in which one African-American was killed and many more injured before the National Guard could restore calm. In 1980, two members of the Ku Klux Klan shot four black women, but a white jury acquitted them — sparking the firebombing of several businesses.

With so many jobs lost and racial tensions high, it was obvious the traditional response in American cities — a few leaders snapping their fingers, ordering up a new technology, bulldozing some slum blocks — wouldn't work.

Civic intervention begins

Enter concerned civic leaders, including Rick Montague, director of the Chattanooga-based Lyndhurst Foundation, Gene Roberts (later to become mayor) and Mai Bell

Hurley (who would subsequently head the famed Chattanooga Venture process). In the early 1980s, they began public meetings — 65 in all — to listen to people's fears and good ideas.

Chattanooga's civic entrepreneurs, with Lyndhurst funding, invited in consultants from far and wide — anyone they thought might have good ideas. Festivals and events to restore confidence in the downtown were begun. Some 50 cities nationwide were surveyed for new civic enterprises. Indianapolis was picked for a city visit. Fifty business, civic and non-profit group leaders joined local elected officials to make the trip. They saw how another community was attempting revitalization; they got to know each other better; they returned ready to invent an approach just right for Chattanooga.

Visits to other cities would, in time, become a Chattanooga institution.

Venture is born

Chattanooga Venture's "Vision 2000" soon emerged. It was preceded by a community survey that revealed Chattanoogans saw the city's greatest assets as its natural beauty, its river location, its mountains and public life. The perceived weaknesses: we're "down" on ourselves, have lost our self-confidence, are divided by race and class.

The 1,700 citizens who took part in Chattanooga Venture, a good social and racial cross-section of the city themselves, were told every idea they wrote down would be seriously considered. An avalanche of ideas was boiled down to 40 truly usable ones, with a strong emphasis on downtown Chattanooga as the place participants held in common, encompassed memories from past generations, made their community special.

The evidence of Vision 2000's success is all over Chattanooga today — financed not just by Coca-Cola heir Jack Lupton's Lyndhurst Foundation, but by major investments by banks and insurance companies in renovating classic late 19th and early 20th century office buildings.

A center with sense of place

Reviewers have given high marks to the handsomely

Until all this civic stirring took place, a big proportion of high school graduates expected to have a last view of Chattanooga in their rear view mirror. Informal recent surveys show a dramatic turnaround, with almost all planning to stay. Asked why, students talk about being challenged and invited to take part in community activities— not ignored, on the sidelines, as in so many places.

renovated Tivoli Theater and the Riverwalk, a set of walkways, plazas and fountains connecting the Hunter Museum, and the handsome new Tennessee Aquarium. On one slope, the architects even included a set of charming landscaped switchbacks reminiscent of San Francisco's best.

There's also whimsy that reinforces central Chattanooga's sense of place. Consider the once-threatened, now restored Walnut Street Bridge. The community invested $4.5 million to save this century-old iron truss bridge from the wrecker's ball, turning it into a bicycle and pedestrian walkway. Architect Garnet Chapin had the old landmark's iron girders painted a deep happy blue. He included lots of benches where citizens flock, sitting in the sun. He had chrome, contemporary style lamps mounted along the walkways to form a pathway for nighttime strollers; from a distance, they form a charming necklace of light.

"We believe working together works."

—*Chattanooga Chamber of Commerce President James G. Vaughan Jr.*

Audacious housing goals

There has been a major effort to assure Chattanooga's comeback is for everybody. In the mid-80s, spurred on by James Rouse and his Enterprise Foundation, Mayor Roberts and other leaders promised to transform Chattanooga's slums, making all housing units in the city "fit and livable" within a decade. That goal has not been achieved, but Chattanooga Neighborhood Enterprises (CNE) is assembling $23 million a year in foundation money, government grants and low-interest loans by local banks. The result: a powerful wave of repair and renovations. Almost 500 renters are being turned into homeowners each year. CNE aims to raise that to 1,000 yearly, a phenomenal figure for a small city.

It's surely true that latent racial animosities, poverty, school problems, and unequal opportunity still exist in Chattanooga. Miraculous social integration hasn't occurred. Yet the totality of revival efforts seems to have fostered the sense of a community that truly cares about its citizens.

Until all this civic stirring took place, a big proportion of high school graduates expected to have a last view of Chattanooga in their rear view mirror. Informal recent surveys show a dramatic turnaround, with almost all planning to stay. Asked why, students talk about being challenged and invited to take part in community activities — not ignored, on the sidelines, as in so many places.

Of the 40 goals Vision 2000 approved in 1984, 37 had been partially or wholly completed by 1992. In 1993, Chattanooga Venture facilitated a repeat — ReVision 2000, in which some 2,600 citizens generated 2,559 ideas, focused into 27 new goals for the community.

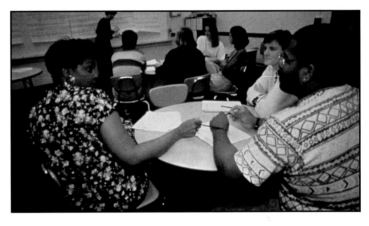

Chattanooga ReVision 2000.   Photo Credit: Chattanooga News Bureau

The sustainability push

In 1995, Chattanooga persuaded the President's Council on Sustainable Development to meet in the city. Even more seriously, it has made a kind of secular religion of achieving sustainability in its own development. And why? Chattanooga Chamber of Commerce President James G. Vaughan Jr. gave the answer to a Chautauqua Conference on Regional Governance in June of 1997:

"Because the old strategy — low taxes, low cost of land and construction, low wages and cheap power — wasn't working any more. We believe some things must grow — jobs, productivity, income and wages, profits, capital and savings, information, knowledge, education. And that others must not— pollution, waste, poverty, energy and material use per unit of output."

And, Vaughan added:

"We believe working together works — supporting collaboration, planning and community building will lead to better decisions, more positive change.... And we believe access to high-quality and lifelong formal and nonformal education will

enable citizens to understand the interdependence of economic prosperity, environmental quality and social equity — and prepare them to take actions that support all three."

Just rhetoric?

One wonders if this is just rhetoric. Yet there are indications it isn't. The Chattanooga Chamber has fought bigger freeways and more downtown traffic lanes. "They're like thinking you're doing something about obesity when you buy bigger clothes," notes Vaughan. The Chamber also opposed local wood chip mills for failing to make either economic or environmental sense.

Designing citizens' way

In 1996, the Chamber devoted its annual planning session to suburban sprawl and the fact that local ordinances often make mixed use development difficult, require too much parking or limit infill development. It supported Futurescape — a program that surveyed some 3,000 citizens on the kinds of streetscapes, developments, and commercial areas they like, based on a visual preference survey devised by urban designer Anton Nelessen. Then the Chamber moved behind an effort to rewrite local ordinances and codes to encourage the kind of development citizens want, and discourage the kind they don't want.

Chattanooga's economic strategy, by the mid-1990s, focused heavily on sustainable development. The city, for example, wanted a circulation system that would stop the pressure to build more unsightly downtown parking lots. So it built new garages on both ends of the downtown and planned a circulator bus system. Then it sought zero-emission vehicles — and found only one U.S. manufacturer of electric buses. The solution? The community started its own company (Advanced Vehicle Systems). Now it has the biggest electric bus fleet in the country, and it's the largest manufacturer.

United Nations recognition

All of this began to attract a collection of remarkable awards. Topping the list: recognition by the United Nations as one of the world's 12 "Best Practice Cities" at the 1996 Habitat II Conference in Istanbul.

Some communities might, at such a point, rest on their laurels. But not, apparently, Chattanooga. In 1997, it accomplished a merger of the city and county school districts, set high student standards and embraced a program aimed at having all children ready to learn by the time they reach school — "the essence of sustainability," Mai Bell Hurley claimed.

Chattanooga was also focusing on a so-called Southside Project, a 400-acre brownfield redevelopment close to center city, to demonstrate sustainable development through a mixed use of housing, low emissions manufacturing, a trade center, a conference and education center, even a small stadium. Simultaneously, City Councilman David Crockett and others were starting to organize an Institute for Sustainable Cities and Companies, focused on training local, national and international leaders in sustainable development's best practices.

The Search for the New Civic DNA

THE KEYS TO SUCCESS in the leadership of American communities have been recast by the rapidly-changing global environment.

Everyone's seen the dramatic changes and begun to feel their effects. The Berlin wall is down. Trade is moving to a no-barriers world. Measured electronically, the globe is now about a half-second wide. The Internet, e-mail, faxes, and satellite hook-ups have cancelled out nation-state barriers to communication. Some $1.3 trillion moves through global currency exchanges each day, with minimal government control.

Globalization opportunities - and perils

Globalization presents opportunity mankind has rarely if ever seen before — to effect scientific and cultural breakthroughs, create new economies, combine skills and create new opportunities across continents. But globalization also can be a menacing force. It tears away the protective envelope of time and space that used to protect inefficient industries and workers with limited skills. It can spell ruin for individuals, corporations and societies that don't compete effectively.

No force comparable to globalization has emerged to sweep away old ways, inefficiencies in government, or outmoded terms of the social contract. There's a deep mismatch between the level of challenges and the way American society is organized, collectively, to deal with them. Historically, we invoked government — federal, state, municipal — to deal with many of our problems, from building railroads or an interstate highway system to social services.

A new order: global, regional, neighborhood

The new level of challenges is quite different: it is global, regional, and neighborhood.

Global because critical impacts are worldwide — global warming, for example, but especially worldwide economic restructuring as it tears apart comfortable relationships.

There's a deep mismatch between the level of challenges and the way American society is organized, collectively, to deal with them.

Regional because metropolitan areas — we call them citistates — are the true cities of our time. They are the real labor markets, the functioning economic communities, the commute-sheds, the environmental basins.

And *neighborhood* because that is where people live, where place and relationships matter more than politics. Neighborhoods are the building blocks of a successful region; if they are weak and socially unstable, a dark shadow is thrown across the entire citistate future.

Regions on their own

The last years have seen a withering of the federal government — not because of the failure of capitalism, but its success. Multinational corporations are showing less willingness to pay for the trappings of the nation state. A politics of austerity and social retrenchment pervades federal and state politics, accentuating America's historic, deep distrust of government. Washington, struggling with its deep debt and seeking balanced budgets, has made discretionary spending its first target. As times change and political pendulums swing, the federal role could, of course, begin to expand again. But when it does, America's regions will be much more connected to and dependent on global connections.

Indeed, an exciting search is on to discover a new civic DNA, the biochemistry of leadership that fits the demands and opportunities of the 21st century.

The bottom line: citistate regions — and neighborhoods — are increasingly on their own. Regional and local leadership — shared across the civic, business and government sectors by people willing to cross the old and familiar boundaries — is more critical than ever.

New leadership form

And in fact, a new form and approach to leadership has been taking shape in the crucible of global-era realities. It is seen most clearly in corporations; it is becoming the hallmark of successful regional communities. The outlines of the shift have been sketched out by the Eisenhower Leadership Group at the University of Maryland. As that project noted in a 1996 report, *Democracy At Risk:*

"In the past, leaders were special people who did special things. The rest were followers who simply went along with what the leader said, and did. The approach seemed to work: if the industrial age was characterized by anything, it was by hierarchical organizations with leaders who were top

executives, and everyone else was down below.

"But today we share a planet that is shrinking. The rules of engagement that applied for most of what has been called 'the American century' no longer work. In the next century, new ways of thinking about leadership will be required, spurred by technology and globalization.

"Organizations will have to be flattened. Leaders and followers are linked and must be involved in the leadership process. Teamwork and collaboration will work better than command and control.

"The new model of leadership is collaborative, requiring widespread participation and collective decision-making. It accepts the inevitability of conflict, but encourages consensus. It searches for win-win solutions.

"This is not to say the new model diminishes the contribution of individuals. Rather it argues that any individual, located any place in the system, can play a leadership role.

"The new model of leadership insists on the participation that is at the heart of the democratic enterprise. The new model confirms that to collaborate is to prepare for civic engagement."

From hierarchy to networks

Douglas Henton of Collaborative Economics emphasizes networking among civic entrepreneurs, leaders from every walk of business, public, civic life, as the key of the new model. The fundamental shift of our time, he says, is "from the centralized, vertically integrated model of business and government dominant in the New Deal and Cold War eras toward a more decentralized, horizontal, and networked regional model."

This is precisely what boundary crossing is all about.

Indeed, an exciting search is on to discover a new civic DNA, the biochemistry of leadership that fits the demands and opportunities of the 21st century.

In the spirit of John Gardner, who inspired this project, the chapters which follow are organized as Gardneresque admonitions — *"the agenda gets tougher," "no one's excused,"* and the like. In most cases these are not the precise words of John Gardner, but they do reflect the philosophy of the grandest civic entrepreneur of them all.

Lesson 1: *The table gets larger — and rounder.*

Everyone knows the classic form of decision-making in American cities. It didn't matter much whether the issue was a convention center, an airport location, a quest for a sports team, or helping the symphony pay off its deficit. A few men, most with white hair, gathered around a starchy white-clothed table at an exclusive downtown club. Without benefit of complex studies, unconfused by hearings or referenda, free of eavesdropping media, the gentlemen were able, somewhere between the appetizer and the Havanas, to cast the die and pledge the resources (theirs and sometimes the public's). The outside world got informed — later.

Indeed, even as the world becomes fast-paced and competitive in a way we never knew before, political gridlock and community stagnation threaten as never before.

The process was efficient, the accountability clear, the implementation quick. But in a globalized era, it doesn't work any more.

The Absentocracy

In the words of *Governing* magazine publisher Peter Harkness: *"The local newspaper used to be owned by local people. The owners of the local TV station, the bank, the major retail stores, the major industries, lived in the community."* But no longer. More often these days, Harkness suggested, *"Gannett owns the local paper, Capital Cities the TV station, Wal-Mart the biggest retail store. Banks are owned by Charlotte or Chicago, local factories by people from some other country."*

Managers of these enterprises are often on temporary assignment, itching for advancement elsewhere. There's not much chance they will invest much of their time or effort, or corporate funds, in the community. The result: loss of people who care for the long haul. We may have criticized them for monopolizing power, but they were an important pillar of American communities' civic order.

The old way has not disappeared everywhere: in some communities a small circle (especially people with their own money to invest) make critical decisions. Yet every group today discovers that if its idea, its latest proposal is a really big one, politics will threaten to shoot it down. Old downtown establishments, racial coalitions, universities, and developers all face that peril. Indeed, even as the world becomes fast-paced and competitive in a way we never knew before, political gridlock and community stagnation threaten as never before.

Contrasting city models
Various regions are at differing points on the continuum from old to new styles. Consider several of those focused on for this report:

Kansas City's gang of four
Kansas City is a model of upper tier organizations working in tandem— Civic Council representing the top 100 corporate leaders, Chamber of Commerce, Community Foundation and Mid-America Regional Council (a council of governments). This group essentially decides the areas the region will focus on, where money goes, and which needs get addressed. Kansas City also has an immense network of block clubs, neighborhood organizations, and community development corps — arguably more, in the aggregate, than any other community in the country. Now there are entries like the Kauffman Foundation, bringing significant new resources and a commitment to convening and collaboration.

Yet there's a feeling that Kansas City's entire civic system fails to function in tandem. Communications between the top four and other groups is very imperfect. There's no single table. In the words of one local observer, "We have many ornaments, but no tree."

Country Club Plaza's J.C. Nichols Fountain
Photo Credit: Bruce Mathews/Convention & Visitors Bureau of Greater Kansas City

Cleveland's network

Cleveland has perhaps the strongest network of civic, community, religious and non-profit organizations anywhere in the country. Examples: the 73-year old Cleveland Community Foundation, America's first community foundation, and the George Gund Foundation, another partner in activist outreach to convene civic forces and deal with serious community challenges over decades. Cleveland Tomorrow, formed in the early 1980s, is a strictly business group — only CEOs sit on the board. But it's not only worked to promote business growth but expanded its purview from Cleveland's successful downtown revival to heavy-duty assistance for the neighborhoods through an affiliate, Neighborhood Progress, Inc.

On top of that, there's the Greater Cleveland Roundtable focused on human relations, Build Up Greater Cleveland to coordinate and boost infrastructure development, the Cleveland Community-Building Initiative to attack poverty in depressed neighborhoods, the century-old Citizens League of Greater Cleveland with its broad government reform agenda — and the list goes on and on.

But is the table big enough for all players— and real participation by all? Some critics have cried "no" for years, attacking shortchanging of the neighborhoods. The issue remains an open one.

Atlanta: Olympic breakthroughs

The business of Atlanta, people say, is business. The traditional business leadership had a kind of plantation attitude toward the city's large low-income African-American population. But Maynard Jackson, elected Atlanta's first black mayor in the 1970s, refused to follow the business agenda. He established, for example, 24 Neighborhood Planning Units (NPUs) to review planning, land use and city budget decisions — a form of mini-neighborhood government for traditionally ignored areas. Andrew Young, succeeding Jackson as mayor, spoke a language of economics and global connections that business liked.

So it was that the audacious idea was raised — that Atlanta might capture the 1996 Olympics, transforming

Atlanta's Vision 2020
Photo Credit: Atlanta Regional Commission

the city's image and creating a springboard into the 21st
century — and that the right alliance was in place. "It
wasn't the Olympics that taught us how to work together," said Atlanta Regional Commission director
Harry West. "We were able to get the Olympics because
we had learned to work together." Or in the words of
Shirley Franklin, at various times chief operating officer
of the city and managing director of the Atlanta Committee for the Olympic Games: "Maynard brought the
neighborhoods to the table with the NPUs. Andy
brought business back to the table. By the 1990s, everyone was at the table."

The prospect of the Olympics putting Atlanta on the
world stage gave the often desperately poor black
neighborhoods in the city's "Olympic Ring" of inner city
areas a chance to demand long-overdue changes. It was
clear enough that wretched slum conditions, virtually in
the shadow of the Olympic Stadium, would not provide
good press and could become a gross embarrassment.
By the time of the Olympics, major projects had been
launched as a result of neighborhood initiatives in all the
affected areas.

Even while so much civic energy was going into the
Olympics, another project of extraordinary scale was
underway — the Vision 2020 project led by the Atlanta
Regional Commission and chaired by a high-profile,
high-energy leader in former Governor George Busbee.

*"Maynard brought the
neighborhoods to the table
with the NPUs. Andy
brought business back to
the table. By the 1990s,
everyone was at the table."*
—*Shirley Franklin
Managing director
of the Atlanta Com-
mittee for the
Olypic Games*

Busbee would tell anyone that he's a political player from the old civic action model, accustomed to devices like blue ribbon committees and getting decisions rapidly.

But in the regional visioning, Busbee found himself counselled to "bring all the partners to the table" in a broadly inclusionary process. He at first resisted, but finally was persuaded. It was, he noted, "a bottoms up planning process, bringing everyone to the table. We had 100 forums throughout the region, and three hour television programs, and questionnaires in the Atlanta newspapers with over 100,000 responses. I thought I knew what everybody wanted. I never believed so many people were that interested in planning their future."

Despite the impressive scale of the 2020 process, many Atlanta leaders thought it left a very light footprint — evidence of how difficult it often is to gain public attention for civic visioning, and how necessary repeat efforts may be.

Portland leads

If there's one place in America where citizen participation is both custom and high art, it is Portland, Oregon. There is "an expectation of participation," according to Metro Executive Director Michael Burton. "It always starts with neighborhood organizations."

Indeed, the 1972 Downtown Plan, which was to form the base for Portland's much-heralded revival and recovery, had its roots in a citizens advisory committee. Citizens were consulted extensively on all the projects, including the McCall Waterfront Park that replaced an ugly riverfront expressway, the flowering of a remarkably well-designed and revived center city, and development of regional light rail transit. Any citizen was free to join one of the subcommittees dealing with such topics as parking, waterfront development, housing and retailing.

The pattern of citizen participation has actually expanded over 20 years. The Portland 2040 Plan, an attempt to plan regional growth to accommodate one million more people, involved extensive community workshops and thinking through of alternatives.

Questionnaires went to more than 500,000 households, asking residents about real choices: whether they wanted more development on transit lines (83 percent said yes), encouraging growth centers (77 percent yes), reducing new lot sizes (58 percent yes), and reducing commercial parking (55 percent).

The bottom line is that people know they belong to Portland, the city and region, because it's become part of the culture for them to be consulted at every step.

Reaching new players
Yet in all communities, there's a problem with outreach, the efforts to expand the discussion table. Just as chambers of commerce sometimes miss significant but just-emerging firms, the formal civic processes tend to leave out the new players. Usually they just don't know they exist.

The "omitted" can be all sorts of types. Some may be founders and operators of new businesses, individuals operating on a global, technological platform who simply haven't seen the relevance of the local scene to their future.

*Communities appear to function best when **each** sector is strong—and learning to pay attention to others and collaborate. Our colleague John Parr may have put it best when he said: "A lot of people need a good listening to."*

Others may be left out because they create uneasiness in mainstream groups. Activists in the Industrial Areas Foundation (IAF) movement (followers of the tradition of Chicago organizer Saul Alinsky) are a case in point. They're rarely dressed in suits; they don't talk the same language as government officials or policy wonks. They insist on confronting deep unfairness and moral ambiguities; they bring up the possibilities of radical change. Not by accident, they usually do their organizing in and with churches in lower-income areas.

"A good listening to"
As Sister Consuelo Tovar of Project Quest in San Antonio explains, IAF-type organizations, lacking money or powerful position, use confrontation and exceptional organization to capture seats at the table.

As democratic expectations rise, as America becomes ever more multi-cultural, the early 21st century is guaranteed to see demands for bringing multiple groups of the disenfranchised and the merely-not-noticed into leadership circles. The trick will be to maintain the interest and commitment of traditional business and civic forces, even while new voices are heard and power broadens. Communities appear to function best when **each** sector is strong — and learning to pay attention to others and collaborate. Our colleague John Parr may have put it best when he said: "A lot of people need a good listening to."

Lesson 2: *The only thing more challenging than a crisis may be its absence.*

When you hear people talking about success in today's cities or regions, most often they're talking about "comeback" stories — some latter-day Lazarus waking from the dead, a regional phoenix rising from misfortune's ashes.

Cleveland would certainly qualify for this distinction. To the nation, Cleveland was the "mistake by the lake." Cleveland became a national laughing stock as a clash between a brash young mayor and the business establishment drove it off the bankruptcy cliff on December 15, 1978, and the Cuyahoga River caught on fire from saturated pollution. It was do or die, and a mobilized business and civic community did a lot.

Cleveland flashback
A flashback to 1920 would have found Cleveland parlaying its strategic location for commerce and transportation into top-tier status — the sixth largest city in America. Growing business gave birth to one of the richest arrays of cultural institutions anywhere — the Cleveland Orchestra, the Cleveland Museum, the Cleveland Play House, the Cleveland Institute of Music, to name a few. The same Cleveland era produced the nation's first community foundation and one of the country's first United Ways.

Hit hard but undaunted by the Depression years, Cleveland prospered from World War II, bouncing into the modern era with a commanding collection of Fortune 500 companies. The population swelled to almost a million by 1950. No one knew it then, but that was the peak.

Over the next three decades, Cleveland would lose almost two-thirds of its manufacturing jobs. Rejecting a metropolitan form of government in the late 1950s, it became an increasingly divided place by race and class. Freeways ripped through vulnerable neighborhoods. School desegregation orders and relentless racism created separate worlds of white and black. The Cleveland that had been such a source of civic pride all came apart in the late 1960s, with the riots and burning that started in the Hough neighborhood. And there was no running from rampant pollution. The "best location in the nation" had become a national embarrassment.

William Seelbach, who first headed Cleveland Tomorrow, the organization that led the effort to bring Cleveland back to prominence, laments the debacle: "Cleveland had been so strong. People got lazy. They took things for granted. Slowly, things broke down." The reason may be, as Thomas Campbell, a retired Cleveland State University historian puts it, that "Cleveland's leaders made the mistake of believing their own propaganda."

From fires and bankruptcy was forged one of the better comeback stories of the 20th century. But not until crisis covered every corner of denial and apathy.

Crisis, Chattanooga and Denver

The story of Chattanooga was much the same — a town that through gross air pollution, rapid industrial loss, and an element of severe racial antipathy, suddenly recognized it was in dire straits. Then, through its civic leadership, it capitalized on that crisis to make an historic comeback. An effort of the breadth of Chattanooga Venture would have been unimaginable without the clear crisis the community faced.

Denver, the fabled American region of the high Rockies, saw its economy go a mile low in the 1980s. Its dependence on the energy business showed when oil prices plummeted and Exxon shut down the oil shale project. Almost overnight, 28,000 energy-related jobs evaporated. Following them into oblivion were more than a dozen industrial banks, and three large savings and loan institutions. The downtown that the boom had built

"Cleveland had been so strong. People got lazy. They took things for granted. Slowly, things broke down."

—William Seelbach,
First President of
Cleveland Tomorrow

was so vacant that jokes were made of how many mountain views one could see through the empty buildings.

It was crisis that spurred Denver's business community and local governments to act. Without a crisis, would downtown Denver have drifted slowly into a Detroit condition? Would anyone have run for office, as Federico Peña did, imploring people to "imagine a great city?"

Detroit turnaround

Or consider the Detroit region. It reluctantly serves as the stereotype of a region in chronic crisis. Nearly every adversity that could befall a major city happened there — from the competitive meltdown of its jewel, the American automobile industry, to urban flight that created the most hollowed out core of all American cities, leaving in its wake hundreds of acres of urban wasteland. For years in the 1980s and early-90s, Detroit failed to register a single housing start. And the racial animosity, Detroit vs. its suburbs, Mayor Coleman Young vs. his white suburban government peers, reached rare levels of vitriol.

Detroit's "Clean Sweep '97": Mayor Dennis Archer (left)
Photo Credit: Hugh Grannum/City of Detroit

So the stage was set for Dennis Archer, the collaborative-style mayor elected in 1993, and for his business and civic allies in the new Detroit Renaissance. Could anyone have credibly suggested they were manufacturing reasons for strategic civic action? Hardly. Everything they've done has sprung from a continuing sense of crisis and necessity.

No crisis: like a frog in boiling water

But in a strange sense, crisis is the easy way. The going's actually tougher when people believe things are pretty much OK. Like a frog in an open pan, too complacent to make his strategic leap until the fire below has brought the water to a boil and he's cooked, many regions of our country bask in a blissful denial that they are severely challenged by changing world conditions or threatened by their own local practices.

The absence of a coalescing crisis keeps them vulnerable.

St. Louis dilemma

St. Louis, like Cleveland one of the premier American cities in the early 20th century, is a ready illustration. Talk to people in most parts of the St. Louis metro area and you inevitably hear about the good life — the lovely, but affordable housing, the Botanical Gardens topping out a list of impressive cultural institutions, the expansive, wooded Forest Park, the easy accessibility to water and wilderness recreation. The conclusion seems inescapable: this must be an exceptionally fine place to live and work.

Take a closer look at the St. Louis situation, and it's difficult to be reassured. The center city population is down a half million since the 1950s and still plummeting — the most rapid decline of major U.S. cities. At the current demolition rate, not a single building will be left in downtown St. Louis by 2020. The region's sprawl index — population growth compared to fresh land devoured — is close to the nation's worst, creating almost insurmountable funding demands for highways and other infrastructure. Jobs are slipping out of the center and corporate headquarters out of the region. City-suburban income differentials are very high. But life's so good for so many people that these issues don't dominate most civic talk. Not yet at least.

San Diego saga

Sunbelt complacency can be a peril too. Journalist-historian Neil Morgan explains how San Diego was formed by Midwesterners and Southerners who loved constructing a cul-de-sac civilization, set apart by the geography of mountains, ocean and desert. They tended

The going's actually tougher when people believe things are pretty much OK. Like a frog in an open pan, too complacent to make his strategic leap until the fire below has brought the water to a boil and he's cooked, many regions of our country bask in a blissful denial that they are severely challenged by changing world conditions or threatened by their own local practices.

to reconstitute their Midwestern and small Southern society. Starting in the 1980s, the bottom began to fall out of the cul-de-sac. The fate of immigrants coming across the border became a hot point of contention. The Navy pulled most of its installations out of town. And there were some model responses, including work to attract smaller high-tech firms to town and Dialogue, a civic process focused on emerging problems like airport location and better trans-border relations in the emerging San Diego-Tijuana citistate.

Still, raw hostility to immigrants continues in many parts of the population. Listen to San Diego talk radio and the issues of strategic choices and shared community futures are inaudible. Even community leaders acknowledge that a full community discourse on San Diego's future, in this island of mild weather and striking scenery, "just isn't happening."

Turnaround — Portland first

Some regions do, however, manage to act in the absence of a precipitating crisis.

The people of the Portland region, a quarter century ago, merely saw crises looming — loss of farm and open space, the exquisite Northwest environment, and a peril of highways devouring the region's preeminent city. They responded with a regional government to match a new state law and set a serious boundary for the urban region. They reduced incentives to drive by killing the proposed Mt. Hood Freeway and replacing roaring traffic arteries with a three-mile long park along the Willamette River. Neighborhoods and architects took strong exception to downtown garage-building and agitated for what became the Downtown Plan that has made Portland into one of the most attractive, vibrant cities on the North American continent.

Indeed, Portland is so sought-after that hundreds of thousands of people from other regions are now pouring in, providing a crisis of how to accommodate the waves of people and new industry without giving up the region's special qualities. Yet Portland wouldn't be wrestling with the problems of success if the people hadn't seen potential crisis and acted in good time. Farmers and foresters saw the peril of creeping urbanization taking over their lands and livelihoods. Citizens and neighborhoods decided the city is theirs. Even today, with new growth pressures, the people of the Portland region seem intent on defining the limits and basic character of the urbanization of their environment — something still quite rare in America.

Charlotte — ahead of the curve

Charlotte, North Carolina also has made a practice of dealing with problems before they turn into crises. There's something in the Charlotte culture that suggests action, forethought, boldness. The town's world-class bankers epitomize the breed. But one finds the same determination to stay ahead of the curve among neighborhood leaders, too. Here is a community that does manage to act in the absence of severe crisis.

In the 1970s, Charlotte was ahead of most communities in effecting quiet but effective school integration. And in the 90s, the city government did something quite important in American life. It set out to take neighborhoods seriously without race riots or social upheavals to force the issue. Finding its traditional hierarchies and department structure could not respond to the needs of a group of quite poor, crime- and welfare-plagued neighborhoods, the city government effected total reorganization. It instituted interdepartmental teams and actually placed priority for funding and special efforts on the poor neighborhoods. The change was accomplished so quietly that the local newspaper, one of the best in America, didn't even notice until it was nearly a *fait accompli.*

It was in Charlotte, too, that 30 neighborhoods ringing the center of the region came together — black and white, rich and poor — declaring their "interdependence" and making a commitment to work together so that the whole community moves ahead. Just mention such an alliance in most regions and you get a wondering stare.

Portland and Charlotte, on opposite ends of the American continent, seem to have learned something systematic about being ahead of the crisis curve. Each demonstrates that a few committed people can lead their region to attempt something, and if it works, to build on it. Leadership needs to come both from the top and from engaged citizens, in ordinary neighborhoods, who move

Portland and Charlotte, on opposite ends of the American continent, seem to have learned something systematic about being ahead of the crisis curve.

to take real responsibility. Such examples are rare and cry out for emulation, because most American regions remain complacent, starved for a crisis that might ignite change.

Lesson 3: *The agenda gets tougher.*

If physical revival focused on downtowns were the sole measure of communities' fate, many regions could declare the "urban crisis" solved. San Antonio can take intense pride in its Riverwalk and the attractions clustered about it. Baltimore has its sparkling Inner Harbor, including the late developer James Rouse's fabulously successful Harborplace. Denver's Lower Downtown has become a symbol of strategically planned, skillfully executed inner city redevelopment.

Cleveland, the Cinderella comeback city of the 1990s, can now boast to the world of its new entertainment hub on the Flats, Rock and Roll Hall of Fame, Science Center, sports stadiums, restoration of historic live theaters on Euclid Avenue, the resuscitation of Terminal Tower, and the combination of successful retailing with hotels in the center city.

The poverty dilemma

Yet for each city with a revived center, a set of gnawing questions remain: Has the lot of the poor been improved? Has downtown revival reduced poverty in any appreciable way? Have racial and ethnic tensions been relieved, minority entrepreneurship expanded?

The answer is almost uniformly "No." The revival impact is simply not apparent; indeed neighborhoods of extreme poverty have increased in most U.S. cities. "There are 41,000 unemployed black males in this region," points out Cleveland Urban League president Myron F. Robinson. "How are we going to bring them into the mainstream?"

This is not to say collaborative civic work has not had significant impact: Witness, for example, the 136,000 affordable apartments and houses that the Local Initiatives Support Corporation, the Enterprise Foundation and allied national intermediaries, working with local community development corporations (CDCs), have created in 1,940 communities across the country. Almost invariably, serious contributions and tax credit investments by local business leadership have made the progress possible.

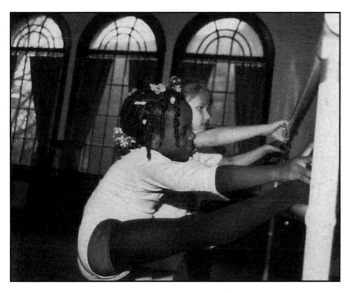

Cleveland's Broadway School of Music & the Arts
Photo Credit: Daniel Milner/Cleveland Foundation

Turnaround breakthroughs

In a handful of individual neighborhoods, intensive efforts by local civic forces and CDCs have begun to produce stunning turnarounds — in Baltimore's Sandtown, for example, and Hough in Cleveland. But in most cities, the yearly reported new abandonments of housing units dwarf anything community redevelopers have been able to achieve. (Example: Detroit in 1996 recorded 86 permits for new residence construction — and 8,432 housing demolitions.)

Fixing any of these problems, civic leaders recognize, will be infinitely more difficult than catalyzing the new downtown towers, convention centers and sports stadiums. Leadership Cleveland titled a recent session "Cleveland — Beyond the Glitz." Proud as they are of recent accomplishments, many Cleveland leaders recognize they have just done the easy part. "We have proven we can build things," says lawyer and civic leader Robert Rawson. "The question is whether we can

"We have proven we can build things," says Cleveland lawyer and civic leader Robert Rawson. "The question is whether we can sustain these partnerships to deal with human needs. To put up a building, you have a plan, you raise the money, and you watch it go up. Dealing with human needs takes more staying power."

sustain these partnerships to deal with human needs. To put up a building, you have a plan, you raise the money, and you watch it go up. Dealing with human needs takes more staying power."

Center cities' financial limits

Can local civic leaders do anything to reverse these trends, the culmination of decades of inner city (and now inner-ring suburban) decline? If the answer is in simple income transfer from public treasuries, the answer is almost surely "no." The large center cities of America, notes the University of Pennsylvania's Anita Summers, are today the caretakers of the nation's poor and immigrants, with significant shares of their budgets already going to cover the costs of poverty — costs most suburban governments bear in dramatically lesser share. Only the national government, and to a lesser degree state governments, argues Summers, can afford to redistribute wealth.

Yet there is little sign that higher governments are willing, under the political conditions of the times, to undertake any kind of redistribution. America's metropolitan regions, by virtue of boundaries set in the 19th century and sometimes even earlier, have in effect compartmentalized their poverty — at the very time globalization is accentuating the income gulf between skilled and unskilled workers. Regions are left with a deepening social overburden that clearly increases public costs and threatens to undermine the economic competitiveness of individual regions and communities.

The hard remaining questions

This is why the agenda for regional leadership has become so much more demanding. The cynics may say that efforts to share taxes, distribute burdens, and break up pockets of intense poverty are too idealistic, doomed to failure. But responsible government, business, and civic leaders will keep returning to the agendas: How do we create a region that is not just economically and environmentally, but also socially sustainable? What can we do to stem capital disinvestment at the core, indeed actually turn it around? What are the ways to encourage the location of new jobs less than vast distances away from existing work forces, including the inner city?

What is the best formula to turn around polluted, idle brownfield sites in cities and older industrial suburbs, so that they can be job-producing locations once again? What new ways can we find to reduce school drop-outs, stem early pregnancies, and prevent an atmosphere of lawlessness in desperate neighborhoods?

One can argue that the sheer necessity of finding answers more creative than traditional income redistribution is coming into focus. The new agenda goes beyond traditional downtown and waterfront renewal to recycling older industrial areas into loft districts for residences, shops, even "cyber-village" growth industries. The new agenda embraces:

* intensive brownfields recycling;
* neighborhood-by-neighborhood economic development planning;
* successful efforts to increase public order through zero-tolerance policing and community policing;
* efforts to find real jobs to replace welfare dependency;
* community insistence on reinvention of local government, especially modernizing inefficient and patronage plagued big city governments;
* school reforms — more and more charter schools, and in cities such as Chicago, shifting direct control and responsibility from school boards to top elected officials.

Solutions have to be regional
What is clear in today's politics is that the core task of reforming public systems, rejuvenating older communities, and introducing new opportunities for low-income neighborhoods must be undertaken on a local basis. And since local municipal lines and rivalries are so often hindrances, and the true human and fiscal resources for reform are regional, the task for initiating, encouraging, and driving change will fall to regional leaders. They need to make the argument for redefining social equity — away from thoughts of handouts to "those people" toward discovering ways to create wealth, even in poor neighborhoods, so that the entire region will bear less of a burden of public dependency, medical subsidies, social

service, police and incarceration costs, and gain more taxpaying citizens in the bargain.

Admittedly, there are some topics so controversial — "third rail issues," as some put it — that extraordinary courage and skill will be required to deal with them. School reform efforts are a case in point: powerful bureaucracies and teacher unions often stand in the path of major change. Another third rail issue: the pervasive issue of sprawling physical development and the multiple environmental and social ills that come in its wake. An obvious solution is the adoption of an urban growth boundary. A few regions, Portland in the lead, have been willing to institute and enforce such boundaries, with very positive results in preserving natural landscape and focusing more development to the urban cores. Yet in most regions, any attempt to institute a growth boundary is quite likely to stir up instant, angry opposition from the powerful development lobby (homebuilders, realtors, title attorneys, mortgage bankers) and the officeholders beholden to it.

Race: still perplexing

There's the ancient, perplexing problem of race — in some regions the continuing saga of white and black, in more and more areas the search for accommodations in a world of exploding ethnic and racial identifications.

The city of Atlanta, and its relationship to the remainder of the Atlanta region, provides a compelling example. The city (now overwhelmingly black) has only 12 percent of the region's population. Once-tiny Gwinnett County, on the northeastern flank of the region, has boomed and now surpasses the city in population. It's another world out in Atlanta's suburbs. This isn't the world of Martin Luther King Jr. and Maynard Jackson. This is Newt Gingrich country. Just 30 miles and a 35-minute drive from where Peachtree Street and Sweet Auburn Avenue meet at Woodruff Park, many people have a hard time understanding how Atlanta matters to their lives. "Most people here would say Atlanta doesn't matter," explains Brenda R. Branch, of the Gwinnett Chamber of Commerce. "But people in the know realize Gwinnett exists because of the city of Atlanta. We know we must be involved in regional issues."

"Regardless of its guise or manifestation," Richard Padgett and James Oxendine wrote in a report for Research Atlanta, "the fundamental reason our metro Atlanta region continues to resist metro-wide approaches to metro-wide problems is race. It is not the only reason, but the overriding, defining reason. No suburb, city, town or county sees benefits in merging its efforts with those of the city of Atlanta. Nor does the city of Atlanta government seek any metro-wide cooperation which will in any way diminish the political or economic power of city government."

Indeed, one discovers a consensus that the major obstacles to Atlanta's continued success come at the intersection of race, political turf, and region. "All of our major problems require regional solutions," according to Leon Eplan, the former Atlanta commissioner of planning and development who played a major role in preparing the city for the 1996 Olympic Games.

Yet the underlying issue is clear enough. "Regardless of its guise or manifestation," Richard Padgett and James Oxendine wrote in a report for Research Atlanta, "the fundamental reason our metro Atlanta region continues to resist metro-wide approaches to metro-wide problems is race. It is not the only reason, but the overriding, defining reason. No suburb, city, town or county sees benefits in merging its efforts with those of the city of Atlanta. Nor does the city of Atlanta government seek any metro-wide cooperation which will in any way diminish the political or economic power of city government."

Racial accord ideas

Not every American region may be as perplexed by race, but there's not a single American metro area where it's not, to some extent, a very real problem. Part of the solution, clearly, is in identifying non-political leaders — in business, civic groups, academia — who can start, in practical and non-confrontational ways, to bring people of varying racial backgrounds together to address problems which they confront in common.

Such an effort was made, on a quite grand scale, with former President Jimmy Carter's Atlanta Project, an heroic effort starting in 1991 to help 20 "clusters" — poor neighborhoods across the city and region — connect with corporate resources. The theory was that the communities would take responsibility for helping themselves. The reality was that the Atlanta Project was perceived as a top-down process led by white-owned businesses, imposing their priorities on black neighborhoods rather than letting cluster communities control their own affairs. With a former president involved, unreasonable expectations were raised. And as President Carter himself explained at a January 1997 conference at the Carter Center: "We thought we could solve in five years problems people hadn't solved in 50 years. The expectations were too high."

Multiple simpler experiments may be the order of the next years. The Center for Greater Philadelphia at the University of Pennsylvania has formed, for example, the Philadelphia High School Partnership: Students United in Service. Over 600 students, in joint teams from over 70 city and suburban high schools, have been brought together to work jointly on community service projects in both the city and suburbs. The avowed goal: "To build personal bridges of trust and friendship over the barriers of race, class and politics that divide."

Hypocrisy half way to virtue

There may also be hope in the amount of talk about the need for collaboration in regions across the country. Regional cohesion, especially in such areas as economic development and environmental sustainability, has become almost fashionable to endorse. And if people's hearts are not always there yet, at least the verbiage around intergroup and regional cooperation may start to yield some fruit. Eventually people do tend to act on some of their rhetoric. Another John Gardner admonition seems appropriate: "Hypocrisy is half-way to virtue."

Lesson 4: *There is no magical leadership structure — just people and relationships*

As leaders in America's regions awaken to the tougher challenges of the global age, a serious, sometimes frantic quest for the right structure follows, almost invariably. Delegations go off to other regions to see how they're organized. The big object: examine the institutions of regions that are doing well to extract the formula for the magical elixir. Faxes fly, phone calls follow. Unashamed to imitate, every region wants to know: what's the best way?

The truth: there's no single formula, no trusty chart, no civic map to follow. Every region does it differently. Just as different flowers flourish in different regions, quite distinct, even contrasting organizational patterns show up as civic successes.

Atlanta learns how

In Atlanta, the scene nearly always shows business driving much of the agenda. Usually, government takes on the role of managing partner. In 1990, having captured the opportunity to host the 1996 Olympics, the Atlanta community moved in typical fashion to create first a private-sector oriented group, the Atlanta Committee for the Olympic Games (ACOG), led by real estate lawyer Billy Payne, the man whose vision and drive had spelled the difference in getting Atlanta selected. The second, the Corporation for Olympic Development in Atlanta (CODA), headed by Mayor Bill Campbell and banker G. Joseph Prendergast, was a semi-governmental entity looking at the civic and community side. Together, these organizations became a prism to see how one region got the widely divergent interests to coalesce around a single mission and its myriad secondary opportunities.

Practically no one in Atlanta questioned that the win for Atlanta had to last longer than 1996. This meant heavy minority participation in the business side of hosting the games. It also dictated quite unprecedented attention to rehabilitating the deteriorating neighborhoods around the downtown. The price of not doing so was obvious — the likelihood of highly negative coverage by an assembled world press.

Beyond the games

What's more, as the late Dan E. Sweatt, former head of Central Atlanta Progress and the Atlanta Project, in 1991 explained the stakes: "We won't emerge in September of 1996 as a world-class city if all we've done is build some stadia and staged some good games and entertained the visitors of the world. If we haven't significantly improved the daily lives of people at the bottom of the economic heap, we won't deserve world-class status."

Atlanta learned how to build relationships among the sectors. "CODA was the bridge," explains Clara H. Axam, CEO of the Corporation for Olympic Development in Atlanta. "There's no way the business executive is going into the neighborhoods. And the neighborhood folk are not comfortable in the board room. CODA could go either place. We learned how to translate conversations to each party. We are the bridge."

The test comes now, post-1996, with Hotatlanta cooled back to earth-bound temperatures: Will the relationships stay connected around that table? Will the community re-building, jump-started by CODA, continue? If so, it will be relationships that make the difference. There's no discernible structure there to lean on.

Denver style

In Denver, despite Western traditions of fiercely defended individualism and intense local independence, it's really government that is expected to lead, because it's the only bridge between the private sector and the community groups that do so much of the work. There, as in most places, leaders of local community groups are inherently ill at ease in the corporate boardroom. And, so is the typical corporate executive in front of a grassroots neighborhood association crowd.

The business community became deeply convinced that major new infrastructure investments were critical to the Denver region's capacity to come out of the recession of the 1980s. Money had to be spent, business leaders believed, even when lots of people had lost their jobs and many businesses were hurting for revenue. Business looked to government to gather the necessary folks around that larger, rounder table.

The final result — a stunning array of new Denver citistate facilities, ranging from the world's largest airport (measured in acres) to a remarkably 21st-century-oriented public library to a neo-nostalgic baseball stadium that ignited a mini-boom in the warehouse district of the Lower Downtown.

Charlotte's special style

In Charlotte, the emphasis on private leadership has been so prominent that the city/county government was radically reinventing its whole organization and nearly no one knew about it. Hard-charging executives such as NationsBank's Hugh McColl have become the prototype of local business leaders taking their region to the national and international competitive tiers.

There are of course the usual business and civic institutions there, including the reinvention of a serious citizens organization — Central Carolinas Choices — but the energy and influence came from more informal arrangements. In fact, during the days when business called all the shots, the CEOs of NationsBank, First Union Bank, the Wachovia Bank, Duke Power, Belk stores, and the *Charlotte Observer*, used to meet to plan projects and allocate corporate giving to community priorities. They called them simply "the Group."

San Antonio and citizen power
In contrast, much of the leadership for change in San Antonio comes from grass roots organizations. There COPS (Citizens Organized for Public Service) and the Metropolitan Alliance organize and train citizens to get the facts about decisions that affect their lives and learn the means of influencing public decisions.

San Antonio is another region with a standard array of organizations, including the Economic Development Foundation of the Chamber of Commerce. But there appears to be no dominating institution, and except for the years that Henry Cisneros was mayor, no dominating political leader to coalesce the community around a mission for change. COPS has a quite respectable record of cultivating productive relationships with key business figures, as they did with Tom Frost, a banker and elder statesman.

But drill the analysis down deeper, and every inch forward toward a better community seems to come largely from the tenacity and talents of people like Consuelo Tovar of San Antonio's Project Quest. She and her organization showed dogged determination in the face of traditional power, daring to say loudly that investing in training for desperately underemployed people is a better use of economic development dollars than tax abatements for new hotels.

Kansas City's gang of four
Kansas City is also a region of strong neighborhood associations and outstanding community development corporations. Most decisions, though, are traceable to the conversations that take place almost daily among the principals of a mere four civic organizations — the Civic Council (the top 100 corporate leaders), the Greater Kansas City Chamber of Commerce, the Greater Kansas City Community Foundation, and the Mid-America

"The secrets to Cleveland's success," says Gund Foundation executive director David Bergholz, "are the talented professionals working in intermediary roles in non-profits, foundations, community development corporations, and city planning agencies." These, he notes, are the people who take the time to build "constellations of trusting relationships" and "serve as the glue between the business and government communities."

Regional Council. This gang of four determines who gets civic money and which projects command priority. It looks like a strength for its clarity, and may increasingly be a weaknesses for its exclusivity, but it's the relationships and the people that govern the agenda.

Cleveland and "trusting relationships"

In Cleveland, one finds major private and community foundations taking a lead role in community development, increasingly in concert with the business community through the CEO-led Cleveland Tomorrow, and the larger local governments. "The secrets to Cleveland's success," says Gund Foundation executive director David Bergholz, "are the talented professionals working in intermediary roles in non-profits, foundations, community development corporations, and city planning agencies." These, he notes, are the people who take the time to build "constellations of trusting relationships" and "serve as the glue between the business and government communities."

Portland excels

Portland is a nearly perfect microcosm of relationship-driven leadership. Over much of the past decade, three women — Barbara Roberts, Vera Katz, and Beverly Stein — once together in the Oregon legislature, became governor, mayor, and commission chair of the largest county. When they acted together, things happened. And they did it often.

At least since the 1960s, Portland has been led by a rare coalition of forward-looking officials, environmentalists, the forest industry, urban planners, builders, business executives, conservationists and farmers. The growth lines they debated and then agreed on have paid off handsomely for the whole region. The 1000 Friends of Oregon comes in for some credit, but so, to a degree, does the Builders Association of Oregon, which eventually saw the merits in more compact growth. The Metro Council in the Portland three-county region keeps the policy framework in tune, but not without the active engagement of nearly every citizen who pays attention to what's going on. Again, it's the people and the relationships that develop.

"At the community level, leaders are made and not born. Building relationships and breaking through barriers are the essential community leadership skills of the next century."

Statue of Portlandia
Photo Credit: City of Portland Office of Neighborhood Associations

Seattle learns from the world

William Stafford, the head of the Trade Development
Alliance in the Seattle region, believes this so strongly
that his program of inter-city visits has taken on breath-
taking scope. In his quest to cultivate the "most interna-
tionally sophisticated local civic group in the world,"
Stafford organizes rigorous study tours to leading global
citistates — among them such places as Amsterdam,
Stuttgart, London, Tokyo, Hong Kong and the Kensai
region of Japan. An average of some 70 Puget Sound
leaders goes on each trip. Many are repeaters, and the
relationships that develop from the experiences and the
conversations have ignited far flung results back home.

Leadership development

Bruce Adams, our colleague on this project, says: "The
leadership lesson is clear — it is going to take many
people from every sector working very hard to turn our
communities around. At the community level, leaders
are made and not born. Building relationships and
crossing boundaries are the essential community leadership skills of the next century."

This kind of relationship building takes place in the
dozens of city-to-city visits and in various city leadership groups throughout the United States each year.
Local leadership groups aim to open participants' eyes
to serious issues. The monthly training sessions range
from education to economic development, health and

human services to the arts. Bankers get to learn about welfare, civil rights activists about job creation, and journalists about the excruciating process of actually making things happen. But the groups' even more critical role is indeed networking—linking emerging leaders, from across the whole spectrum of American community life.

Community foundation potential

In an increasing number of American regions today, the community foundations are playing a convening role, pulling people together, bringing pressure for civic action on long-avoided agendas. With so much civic initiative starved for adequate resources, this may be a propitious point in the role of these organizations. If they can build strong relationships with potential donors, the community-based funds they operate could come to have massive influence. The national philanthropic community is discussing an impending ten trillion dollar intergenerational transfer of wealth in the next few years. If community foundations can tap just a fraction of that money, and then deploy it strategically to seed and increase the civic and creative capacities of their regions, the results could be very exciting.

Meantime, it is futile to imagine some ideal way to proceed, to think that any region has perfected the civic arts to a level that commands imitation.

When a delegation from Atlanta visited the Denver region in the late winter of 1997, there were the persistent, oft-heard questions about organizational solutions — "How do you do it?" The Denverites demurred politely. The explanations, they said, lie in the relationships, not in the structure.

Lesson 5: *No one's excused.*

If cities and regions are more hard-pressed than ever in the new global economy, if bridges across the barriers of race, income and jurisdiction that divide and diminish regions seem a key to a viable future, then who — what kinds of people, what institutions — are available to cope, to help lead in the new era?

Unfortunately, neither governments nor business leaders seem ready to leap into the breach, taking the kind of central leadership that might have been expected of them in the past. Problems ranging from the "absentocracy" (revolving-door leadership, with frequent reassignment to other cities) to bottom-line survival pressures trouble business leadership. Governments are stretched out fiscally and are victims of extraordinarily deep public skepticism.

None of this means business and government will be totally absent partners. The puzzle is: how does the leadership mix get enriched and broadened? How do America's communities tap fresh reservoirs of talent, find newly responsive people and organizations to deal with global-era demands of research, workforce preparation, economic positioning, environmental tradeoffs, and the dilemmas of equity, race and class? Who works to ensure that traditionally underrepresented groups are at the table when it matters? Who thinks about deploying a community's strengths, human and fiscal, in a strategic way? If "the civic enterprise" hired a group of headhunters, where would they first be dispatched?

Our top candidates: universities, professions, faith communities, and the media.

Academic openings
Universities and colleges are arguably the biggest, least tapped, most strategic new leadership sector for America's regions. In an information age, they are the information specialists. Each year, they receive hundreds of billions of dollars of the national wealth, either through tax or philanthropic dollars. And they have crept up on, in many instances replaced, private firms as the biggest players in town. Indeed, in region after region today, the "eds and the meds" — the universities and their hospitals — are *the* largest non-governmental employers.

Universities *could* become critical actors in building the new American society — *especially* at today's critical juncture point when the growing income divisions between haves and have-nots, manual laborers and the professional elite, are becoming so profound and worrisome. Indeed, the growing skills and income division in American society, reflected in the interrelated crises of family disintegration, neighborhood and downtown decay, malfunctioning schools and crime and wasteful sprawl development, is arguably the central intellectual crisis of our time. As such, it's a crisis that our universities, our prime intellectual resources, ignore at their peril.

"Universities," notes Ira Harkavy, director of the University of Pennsylvania's Center for Community Partnerships, "cannot afford to remain shores of affluence, self-importance and horticultural beauty at the edge of inland seas of squalor, violence and despair."

Changing academic culture

After decades of responding to the federal demand for defense-related research, argued President William Greiner of SUNY Buffalo, it's time to take our university resources and turn them to development of human capital. "We train too many PhDs, cloned to be like us. They're smart. But now they need to be trained for national service, to populate the agencies and the schools. It's part of our defense conversion."

Yet there's an ingrained academic culture that is difficult to change. Faculty are encouraged to develop more loyalty to their academic discipline than to the community that sustains them. When seeking tenure, community service is routinely disregarded. The pressures are all to "publish or perish."

Moreover, most American universities' community-oriented research, even when it's thoughtful and inventive, tends to be episodic. Too often it is scorned by fellow faculty as second-rate "applied research," or "lacking in rigor." Holistic research, the type of interdisciplinary work most essential to get to the most fundamental problems of our society today, is too often the orphan.

Reform opportunities

How can the entire university — not just urban affairs or government departments, but the whole academy — become a strong city and regional civic player? How can the focus, from anthropology to chemistry to business management, be on incorporating poor and uninformed people into our society? How can programs be created

---

"Universities," notes Ira Harkavy, director of the University of Pennsylvania's Center for Community Partnerships, "cannot afford to remain shores of affluence, self-importance and horticultural beauty at the edge of inland seas of squalor, violence and despair."

where the university's students, undergraduate and graduate, and its faculty, are in the community working with neighborhood people to create new and effective solutions and approaches?

Some leadership may come from imaginative university presidents and chancellors. Some from far-sighted department chairs and, even more likely, from dedicated individual faculty. The entire regional community needs to remind universities that there are highly successful university-community experiments and projects under-way in communities across America.

Starring examples

Portland State University, for example, played a key role in launching the regional governance concept in the late 1960s and early-70s. Ethan Seltzer, the current director of the Institute of Portland Metropolitan Studies, is a recognized keeper of the regional flame.

Or consider the College of Urban Affairs at Cleveland State University — the linchpin institution of Ohio's state-funded Urban University Program. The effort is mirrored at such other institutions as Ohio State, the University of Cincinnati and Kent State. But the stellar example remains Cleveland's (bolstered by additional funding from the Gund and Cleveland Foundations). For two decades, its university based Urban Affairs Center has done the essential, often breakthrough re-search on the Cleveland region, from housing patterns to poverty to governmental forms. Its longitudinal analy-sis of housing and land use trends, including all of Cuyahoga County and increasingly all of Northeastern Ohio, is arguably the most advanced of any regionally-based university in America. The same institution has undertaken training for neighborhood leaders. As more and more citistates try to make sense of their regional growth patterns, the model deserves study and emula-tion.

Brooklyn's Pratt Institute Center for Community and Environmental Development, started in the 1960s with a grant from the Rockefeller Brothers Fund, provides another example. The Center began by consulting with and working closely with community-based organiza-tions in its own Brooklyn neighborhood. It pioneered the concept of "advocacy planning" done with and for neighborhoods. It defines its mission as assisting "low- and moderate income neighborhood groups to solve community-defined problems by developing community-preferred solutions." Among its services to neighborhoods are needs analysis, comprehensive planning, program development, and project financial packaging. Through high standards and hands-on experience, it has earned its strong professional reputation.

... and more advances

Multiple other examples abound. The outreach effort into East St. Louis of the University of Illinois at Urbana-Champagne is fast becoming one of the United States' premier "best practices" in direct faculty-student-community contact. There is also broad placement of students in community-based projects inaugurated by the Shriver Center at the University of Maryland-Baltimore County. An inter-university collaboration, called Policy Action Research Group, formed by four Chicago area universities — Loyola, DePaul, the University of Illinois/Chicago, Chicago State, has been engaged in more than 130 projects around the region, in every policy area from a local welfare reform effort called "earnfare" to housing rehabilitation to determining what it takes to maintain racially and economically integrated neighborhoods.

In Charlotte, a Regional Assessment Center has been established within the University of North Carolina at Charlotte, watching region-wide developments, creating a regional web page, and considering transportation and growth options. One of the goals is putting proposed major developments on line, allowing citizens to weigh scenarios and alternatives.

San Diego story

Another example comes from the University of California at San Diego. San Diego Dialogue, a bi-national citizen-business partnership, sprang into being in 1991 after Neil Morgan, author and longtime *San Diego Union* columnist, placed a critical call to Mary Walshok, UCSD's activist associate vice chancellor of extension activities. The region, Morgan noted, had no nonpoliticized forum in which people could talk through challenges the region faces.

Walshok reacted and the Dialogue was born. Chaired by William McGill, ex-Columbia University president and UCSD chancellor, it has lived up to its name by sponsoring discussions on every area from border relations to public transportation to education reform. It has moved top San Diego business leaders, many of whom had rarely ventured south of the border before, to learn about joint economic challenges at gatherings with prominent Tijuanan hosts.

The same branch of the University of California at San Diego also founded, in 1985, an organization called CONNECT. The whole idea is to breed and grow start up technology firms by connecting them with faculty research skills and outside corporate investors. The results have been spectacular— in 10 years the number of local biotechnology firms has grown from 44 to 110, communications companies from 36 to 60, computer firms from 35 to 130. CONNECT claims it is now helping local firms net about $600 million in capitalization each year.

Outside pressure needed

One can imagine universities, in the coming years, acting more and more as catalysts for their regions — sponsoring research, seeking out "best practices" for community-based efforts, acting as conveners of regional forums and assisting independent citizens leagues with research and other collegial assistance.

But one suspects it will require constant pressure from community leaders outside the academy, leaders willing to urge broader roles for universities and colleges, to criticize inaction, praise sound new efforts, talk openly about reform of faculty promotion incentives, and to get involvement up to the critically effective level in U.S. communities. Today, the academic sector is simply not pulling its weight.

Beyond universities, there are all sorts of other groups in any regional society who should not be excused in the search for strong regional leadership in a globalized world.

Tapping professions and the faith community

Clearly the trained and valued professions — law, medicine, accounting, architecture and the like — should be challenged on this score.

Consider the faith community — churches, synagogues, temples, and mosques. Collectively, each faith represents a magnificent region-wide community. Each is in a position, through its members, through their informal networks, to exercise significant influence. In any region one will already find highly constructive ways, especially in social action, that at least a number of faith communities are involved.

New levels of activity and new ways of playing a critical regional role are now required. Anthony Pilla, the Roman Catholic Bishop of Northeast Ohio, has tackled the perplexing, immensely difficult issue of suburban sprawl. Starting in the mid-1990s, he suggested to his flock of one million Cleveland-area Catholics that there are deep moral dimensions to the expressways and subdivisions, the fresh strip malls and sewers and utility lines that keep pushing suburbia ever outward. Poorer people in the older cities and suburbs, he noted, become isolated and disassociated from society in the process. Bishop Pilla began to mobilize Catholics to lobby quietly with governments and developers and decision makers, suggesting they look for ways to focus development back more toward the established city and suburban centers, toward a shared regional future.

Consider the faith community — churches, synagogues, temples, and mosques. Collectively, each faith represents a magnificent region-wide community. Each is in a position, through its members, through their informal networks, to exercise significant influence.

The Pilla model — whether on environmental or social issues or both — is especially promising. Faith communities operate regionally; increasingly the problems of our society are also regional. The opportunities for adherents to network across municipal and class lines are legion.

Local foundations also could take an issue such as sprawl and work consciously to get multiple faith communities to recognize the serious stakes, to educate and gain involvement from congregations across the entire region. The leadership role of community foundations is enlarging rapidly as they multiply and grow — but still is only a fraction of its potential, especially in helping regions reach out to new constituencies and to think strategically.

Media — also not excused

If the faith and foundation communities are not to be excused from major regional issues, surely the media should not be either. Newspapers, television, radio may be commercial enterprises. But they enjoy First Amendment rights for a reason. They are a critical link between citizenry, government, and the creation of healthy civic processes.

Commercial local television's common denominator of news programs packed with violence, scandal and the banal represents an assault on the health of the community — one that deserves criticism, in communities nationwide, by responsible civic forces.

Media as community player

But the print media ought not be left off the hook. There are some papers which seem to make a strong, ongoing effort to inform their communities and promote civic dialogue. One of these is the Portland *Oregonian*, whose veteran editorial page leader, Larry Hilderbrand, notes the paper's intent not to polarize issues, "to allow time for the public to understand the implication of decisions." Indeed, the *Oregonian* can be considered one of the authors of Portland's open political culture. Hilderbrand explains Portland's openness to new ideas from rank-and-file citizens with two questions: "How many New Yorkers walk into a newspaper with an idea? Here they do. How many go see the mayor? Here they do."

Yet even the *Oregonian*, community leaders fear, has tended in recent years to move toward shorter, trendier stories of less long-term importance. Over and over again, surveyors for this study heard civic entrepreneurs express keen disappointment over their local press, suggesting it was more of a problem in civic discourse than a force to make the community stronger. The many critics believe newspapers have strayed from their essential civic role: namely, to provide critical information, bolster spirited debate, and help a community discuss alternative solutions to problems. Reporters, they allege, have read and reported from crime blotters instead of interviewing in depth in affected neighborhoods. Editors have overweighted pages to investigative instead of substantive issues journalism. Chain ownership of papers has cut pennies and discouraged crusading. Too many publishers seem to believe their chief mission is delivering audiences to advertisers.

Alarmingly, they divide regions into zoned editions which undermine any meaningful regional debate of critical, shared issues.

Civic journalism frontier

Today's prevailing method of news coverage, asserts Cole Campbell, editor of the *St. Louis Post-Dispatch*, excludes sufficient coverage of women, of minorities, and — with its rush to focus on officialdom, political winning and losing games — even excludes citizens. "You do not see in news reports," Campbell alleges, "ordinary citizens going about the task of deliberating and making decisions and improving their lots in life." Newspapers, Campbell asserts, grasp the moment but not the times. They too often fail to provide a meaningful context in which people can solve the problems of their lives and communities. They fail to see their readers "as an engaged public, not merely a persuaded audience — an engaged public that takes responsibility for what's going on in the community, not simply people who are waiting to be sold on some agenda by political figures, business leaders, or the newspaper's editorial page."

Campbell is prominent among the nation's so-called public or civic journalists, a breed that emerged in the 1990s anxious to give more breadth, less sensationalism, more community-based sensitivity to coverage. Among the leaders were such papers as the *Wichita Eagle, Charlotte Observer*, the *Wisconsin State Journal* and Wisconsin Public Television, the *Tallahassee Democrat, Seattle Times*, and the three winners of the Pew Center for Civic Journalism's 1997 Batten Award — the *Peoria Journal Star*, the *Bradenton Herald* and the *Rochester Democrat and Chronicle*.

Direct challenge strategies

If a community is "stuck" with shallow, winner-and-loser type journalistic coverage, can it influence publishers and editors to do better? The answer has to be yes. Leaders from outside the press, from neighborhood activists to business elite, may well have to take up the matter directly with publishers and editors of their local newspapers, delivering a message like this:

"No one's asking for sugar-coated, boosterish stories.

"You do not see in news reports," St. Louis Post-Dispatch Editor Cole Campbell alleges, "ordinary citizens going about the task of deliberating and making decisions and improving their lots in life." Newspapers, Campbell asserts, grasp the moment but not the times.

What we do want is fair, full, interested coverage of the civic enterprise. To be competitive in the new global economy, we'll need a strong local economy, a sustainable environment, viable neighborhoods, regional cohesion. The vigor and curiosity and sensitivity you give to our struggle can make an immense difference. You're not excused."

Lesson 6: *Sometimes the old ways still work.*

As more people come to accept the reality and necessity of inclusive, participatory civic processes, there has been a tendency to dismiss the idea that individual leaders can make a difference. It almost seems that any mature, white male in a prominent organization should make a discreet entry and look for a low-profile back-row seat. As nearly all the top-down civic hierarchies have faded — the Vault in Boston, the Group in Charlotte, the 8F Group in Houston, the so-called Citizens Council in Dallas, the Phoenix 40 — one would think there's no place for this sort of leadership.

Sometimes, still, there's no substitute for it. Some communities consistently achieve "representativeness" in a civic effort, and nothing else.

The McColl model
There are still occasions when a figure like NationsBank Chairman Hugh McColl of Charlotte — eager to be the first bird off the wire, flying boldly off in a new direction, expecting others to follow — does get things going, does create opportunities for many others to follow. We were talking with McColl in his top-floor office back in 1995, and remember what he said about the northside of downtown Charlotte, looking out the window. The market wasn't reaching to those neighborhoods, where run-down structures and struggling public housing filled most blocks. He said: "We have to do something about that." As it turns out, he intended to buy whole parcels and become the developer to ensure that businesses and new housing found their way to the part of Charlotte's core that the market was too slow to see. Using his influence and resources, McColl started something that many others will finish.

The moral: even as the solo leadership model fades, one should not too soon or easily dismiss what single leaders do.

Charlotte Public Meeting
Photo Credit: Central Carolinas Choices

"But as we construct governing coalitions in the contemporary style — open, inclusive, collaborative — we had better be sure to build into them some of the old virtues: the sense of values, the sense of obligation and trust, responsibility for the community as a whole, that they embodied."

—John W. Gardner

Denver, Atlanta examples

Even the most durable collaborations are often born from the persistent push of one or two old-style leaders. At the depth of Denver's financial woes in the mid-1980s, the Metro Denver Network, a collaborative of public and private entities in the region to do economic development and recruitment together, happened because Richard C.D. Fleming, Tom Clark of the Metro Denver Chamber of Commerce, and one or two business leaders kept pushing for it.

The moral: even as the solo leadership model fades, one should not too soon or easily dismiss what single leaders do. There is no good theoretical case for why Atlanta should have played host to the Olympics. But it got the bid and carried off the games, largely because of the original vision and dogged determination of one attorney, Billy Payne.

Getting the vital push

Even when a region's advances are marked by highly collaborative processes, often one or two individuals gave the vital push, at the ideal moment, to get things rolling. Oregon's decision to eschew new freeways, institute statewide land use planning, and preserve a lively downtown Portland depended on key individual leaders at important moments. The land use law, for example, was largely the work of one farmer legislator, Hector McPherson, acting in collaboration with then-Governor Tom McCall.

It's fair to ask

What if George Voinovich had not succeeded Dennis Kucinich in Cleveland? What if Federico Peña had not challenged the establishment to break the mold and run for mayor of Denver? What if Richard Fleming and the Denver business establishment had not had the nerve to embark on a daring strategy in the midst of a recession?

Gardner on establishments — old and new

John Gardner's own words are best:

"The old establishments had well-known failings that made them unfit for survival, given the trends in contemporary life. They were not open; they didn't hold out a warm welcoming hand to newcomers. They excluded certain groups. They had a rigid, top-down view of how the world should run. They fiercely resisted change.

"In some cities the Establishment had virtues worth pondering. Members had shared values; they had a sense of mutual obligation and trust that enabled them to exercise effective influence as a group. In their dying days, their vices hardened and their virtues decayed.

"But as we construct governing coalitions in the contemporary style — open, inclusive, collaborative — we had better be sure to build into them some of the old virtues: the sense of values, the sense of obligation and trust, responsibility for the community as a whole, that they embodied."

Lesson 7: *Collaboration is messy, frustrating & indispensable.*

Another Gardnerism sets the stage here:

"Behind all the buzz about collaboration is a discipline. And with all due respect to the ancient arts of governing and diplomacy, the more recent art of collaboration does represent something new — maybe Copernican. If it contained a silicon

chip, we'd all be excited. As it is, it's mostly tolerated as just another step in our social bumbling."

While Gardner looks forward, many individuals resist the new, collaborative ways. In the words of one Atlanta business executive: "My idea of a good meeting is just two people — me telling you what to do."

The trouble, of course, is that such a tidy little power trip doesn't log many miles in today's world. Indeed, it's not even viable in the fast-decision world of the corporate sector, where the vestiges of the military model hide from collaborative capture.

Denver is an example of a real "business" town, with as aggressive a record as any in getting things done. Yet even in Denver, no one gets by with deciding something for everybody else. It's all more complicated. As City Council Member Happy Haynes explains:

"Most governments would think long and hard these days before trying a top-down, shove-it-down-the-throat approach. Yet it's a bit too romanticized to say that the old ways have totally disappeared. Those temptations aren't gone. Collaboration is actually very hard work, and not appealing to everybody. But still, when somebody does try to just ram something through, they hear about it, and pay for it. Between the media and citizen groups, it doesn't work that way anymore."

A partnership era
The fact is that interesting forms of partnership and collaboration are behind a vast number of the downtown and neighborhood revitalizations, reformed social service efforts, and environmental accords reported in American regions today. The word partnership dominates descriptions of how such city regions as Cleveland, Indianapolis, Baltimore, Portland and Denver have been able to move forward.

The model is spreading — and taking on new forms. In Virginia, the heavily black city of Richmond and its overwhelmingly white, bigger and richer suburbs scrapped for decades over every issue from poverty to transportation to annexation. Interlaced with racial antagonism, some of the fights were quite bitter. But in

---

===✿===

"Most governments would think long and hard these days before trying a top-down, shove-it-down-the-throat approach. Yet it's a bit too romanticized to say that the old ways have totally disappeared. Those temptations aren't gone. Collaboration is actually very hard work, and not appealing to everybody. But still, when somebody does try to just ram something through, they hear about it, and pay for it. Between the media and citizen groups, it doesn't work that way anymore."

—Happy Haynes
Denver City
Council Member

the 1990s, led by business, leaders in the Richmond area began to take a different view. One object: tackling a 43 percent child poverty rate through new health and anti-violence programs. The Greater Richmond Chamber of Commerce became the lead welfare-to-work agency in a partnership with social service departments in the city and three surrounding counties, pledging to find jobs for 1,700 public aid recipients in little over a year.

Reservations, concerns

A transition process isn't always easy. Gloria Robinson, former planning and development director in the administration of Mayor Dennis Archer in Detroit, describes the agony of transition in the political and civic culture, moving from the trenches of a polarized power struggle to the tables of collaboration and compromise.

There are some nervous that collaboration will be used as a control device. Harold McDougall, Catholic University law professor and one of our colleagues on this project, warns: "Some people have learned to speak the new language of collaboration so they can control the group. You have to call them on it."

Shirley Franklin, who managed the Olympic committee in Atlanta, says she learned that "it's more than just getting to the table, just getting power from white men. It's generational, it's a complex play with power bases, including the black institutional power base. It's across city lines, county lines, sometimes state lines. It covers crime, water, transportation, and every other issue that matters."

Learning "new civics"

It is important to see how camps less accustomed to collaboration — business leaders, for example — learn the game. When Richard Fleming was the head of the Denver Partnership, a new downtown organization, and on the threshold of taking over as CEO of the Denver Chamber of Commerce, he talked about a "new civics." This meant more power-sharing with new players, more consensus-based decision making, greater use of non-profit organizations, more public entrepreneurship, and shrewd market-based strategic planning. The results, as his approach gained acceptance, were stunning. But it was a language of partnership not much known when

A transition process isn't always easy. Gloria Robinson, former planning and development director in the administration of Mayor Dennis Archer in Detroit, describes the agony of transition in the political and civic culture, moving from the trenches of a polarized power struggle to the tables of collaboration and compromise.

Fleming first thrust it into the open civic air in the early 1980s.

Ironically, it is a model of less hierarchical, collaborative behavior — within a corporation, and with key outside contacts — that now pervades advanced corporate thinking. It has now begun to permeate the civic sector with the growth of the group that Douglas Henton, John Melville and Kimberly Walesh — in their book, *Grassroots Leaders for a New Economy* — call the civic entrepreneurs. These are the individuals who learn to work smoothly across sectors, working to develop common approaches that encompass business success, community goals and regional competitiveness. They're found in entrepreneurial businesses, global corporations, economic development agencies, foundations, environmental groups, government, even, on occasion, the media. They mediate between sometimes antagonistic groups, "walking between the raindrops" to create consensus and forward movement.

A more participatory future

John Gardner, at 85 a true national treasure, a man who would head any civic college of cardinals, thinks we're in a transition, welding the assets of our establishment past to a more participatory future. At a meeting in early 1997, he said:

"I think we're trying to put together a new Establishment. It took me a long time to realize this, working to found the Urban Coalition, Common Cause and the like....I was trying to get in things of old — trust, responsibility, things that one would have found in an old town. I was trying to create a new, more diverse and inclusive group, but without losing the trust and sense of responsibility and commitment of old groups. That's what we have to keep on trying. It's long and slow to get people talking across the table with a sense of trust, not seeing that other person as a category, like 'Korean grocer'.... The transition is taking us a couple generations — to reach the further shore of cross-boundary Establishments."

If the process is tough, if results sometimes seem elusive, if there's a price to be paid in time, emotion, and energy — well, who ever said life was easy? Turning again to John Gardner: "If you want the hen to lay, you have to tolerate the cackle."

We do need, in the end, some new establishment, some focus of leadership and direction, says Gardner. "The more that crisis is a creeping variety, like sprawl, the more you need some sort of establishment response."

Lesson 8: *Government always needs reforming, but all the reforms need government.*

Ever since Revolutionary times, we Americans have distrusted and consistently disparaged government. But our healthy skepticism has turned into dangerous cynicism that makes it difficult for our governments to play an effective role in the new global economy. If we shackle government, starve it for truly needed funds, we may get just what we deserve — government mired in the management methods of the 1950s. Since government is at least 15 to 20 percent of any local economy, the entire economy is then shackled and pulled down.
It is a fact that no matter how much business or philanthropies or other civic forces seek to lead, at the end of the day government is needed, almost invariably, as a partner at the table. Any major undertaking runs up against rules, regulations, funding priorities, land use plans or some other domain of government. Local government is needed as a funding partner in major enterprises. It is needed to provide quality services, especially in poor and struggling neighborhoods, and to start the tough task of tying social services for families to school programs in a time of serious family breakdown. It is needed to protect the air and water, and to assure environmental equity to low-income neighborhoods often the scene of landfills or toxic dumping.

In addition, a community that tries to operate independent of government may easily find itself paralyzed when it tries to work collaboratively.

The public will
Government, moreover, does remain the only instrument to effect the public's will in a fully democratic way. Only government has the power to assure true equity in a society. And government, eventually, can lend legitimacy to many vital public efforts.

It is a fact that no matter how much business or philanthropies or other civic forces seek to lead, at the end of the day government is needed, almost invariably, as a partner at the table.

Governance in America's regions is complicated by the public's tendency — fed by the media — to continue focusing on the municipality of the inner city, even while major chunks of the population, not to mention economic muscle, have headed for the suburbs.

Contrasting regional mindsets

Each American region seems to have its own mindset about government. In Kansas City, government is expected to be at the table, even if that's usually someone else's table. In Portland, it is a kind of collective consciousness — the expression of public will. In San Diego, it's the arbiter of relentless growth debates. In Chattanooga, it's proven that archaic form is no bar to civic innovation.

In Detroit, the city government has moved from political machine to racial fortress to would-be innovator in a new striving for regional collaboration. In Denver, notwithstanding the region's open and western image, government is expected to initiate and lead important projects.

Charlotte learns

Charlotte historically revered its big businessmen as the catalysts and arbiters. Charlotte presents the interesting case of a region in which many people failed to recognize government's importance until the mid-90s rise of the social conservatives, when the recognition suddenly dawned: "Oh, government is the way we fund the arts and many other public goals."

Charlotte also has experienced a quite remarkable "quiet revolution" — constant merger of Charlotte city and Mecklenburg County programs and divisions, so that city-county merger may someday simply happen, as opposed to the prolonged and bloody battles that government consolidation would require in most U.S. regions.

Government as bridge among sectors

Another vital role of government in today's cities and regions is as **bridge** between other sectors that seem to have difficulty talking with one another. In such cities as Cleveland, Atlanta and Denver, one finds quite strong lines of communication connecting the business community with the city and other municipal governments.

*Another vital role of government in today's cities and regions is as **bridge** between other sectors that seem to have difficulty talking with one another.*

There's also regular communication between community-level organizations — community development corporations, for example — and the city government. But there's not much direct communication between community leaders and business leaders.

"The reason is hardly mysterious: there is a big culture gap between grassroots communities and business. The challenge is to get the different cultures — government, community, and business — working together in the public interest," notes our project colleague Bruce Adams.

Often, government — through planning departments, through mayors and council offices — is able to provide the missing communications link. Government's ally in providing the missing links is a group of intermediaries — civic entrepreneurs — such as chamber of commerce vice presidents, heads of citizens leagues and directors of community foundations.

Government performance demands
Yet as helpful as government may be in its alliances and communicating role, it also is subject to all of today's pressures of globalization, to prove itself more efficient, and more responsive to its citizens. Clearly, U.S. municipal governments have increased in professionalism over the past decades. Bossism and outright corruption have declined as problems.

Still, there remain pockets of gross inefficiency, red tape, and bureaucratic sloth. Pressure for government reform — the kind of impetus that led to the National Civic League's founding in 1894, and local leagues in many other cities — are as needed now as ever. Bureaucracy creates public hostility and enervates public will. Civil service systems adopted in the Progressive reform era have all too often become albatrosses when governments attempt to change personnel to react crisply to changing demands.

Liberals often defend large-city governments because the cities are home to many minorities and poor. Conservatives tend to react viscerally to criticism of small, suburban jurisdictions. Lost in the shuffle are needed, spirited debates about benchmarks and standards that large urban governments should be expected to achieve.

Another challenge: clear evaluation of the hundreds of hyper-fragmented local governments in many regions. The hard questions need to be posed: How well do they actually perform? Would increased consolidation effect true economies of scale?

Responsive government

A related, growing group of issues revolve about government accessibility and responsiveness to citizen and neighborhood needs. Examples: community policing, brownfields clean-up, downtown management, bureaucratic reorganization to respond to neighborhoods, and making city government functions easily understood and accessible on the Internet.

Today's society obviously wants less bureaucratic, less intrusive, and less dictating government. More than ever, reforms thought up, initiated, and pushed by communities and non-profits and civic forces are essential. Yet in one form or another, each civic effort requires government as an active, smart partner. In the final analysis, there's no other way.

The Alamo—Shrine of Texas Liberty
Photo Credit: San Antonio Convention & Visitors Bureau

Lesson 9: *Place matters.*

We live in a cyber-age, globally connected, our communications systems instant, our corporations functioning across continents. Still, geographic home is vital. If schools are mediocre, or even terrible, if the air or the water is polluted, if the crime rate's high, one knows that place matters. Only portions of a person's life can be spent on jets, on ships, on the road, on the Internet. Home isn't just a nice word; it's central in any kind of practical human life.

Not only do humans need to be grounded, the only practical place to practice civics — the vital act of citizenship — is in a community.

Today, and for the foreseeable future, there are three vital place-based communities: regions, neighborhoods, and center cities (or downtowns).

Regions

Spilling out across the open countryside in seemingly amorphous shape, regions may not, initially, evoke thoughts of "place." But they are, as discussed earlier in this paper, the organic, most important economic and environmental entities of the post-Cold War world.

They are natural communities for two more reasons, starting with their interdependence — what former Housing and Urban Development Secretary Henry Cisneros calls their "interwoven destinies."

Interdependence relates not just to the fact that communities across regions breathe the same air, use the same transportation systems, share the same water, and impact the same natural systems. Their workforces are thoroughly intermingled. Suburbanites use — and in fact own, through various financial institutions — major parts of center city properties. Multiple studies suggest that suburbs are far more likely to prosper when the inner cities are doing well. Leaders in the country's most aggressive regions — from Chattanooga to Cleveland to San Diego — repeat the need to reform faltering inner city schools for the entire region to develop a competitive 21st century workforce.

Multiple studies suggest that suburbs are far more likely to prosper when the inner cities are doing well. Leaders in the country's most aggressive regions—from Chattanooga to Cleveland to San Diego— repeat the need to reform faltering inner city schools for the entire region to develop a competitive 21st century workforce.

... and problem-solving

Regions are natural communities for a second reason: they are the best arenas for problem-solving. Why? Because the critical challenges of our time — from the environment to transportation to economic development to workforce preparedness — seem most comprehensible at a regional scale.

They are important for people's identity, too. Get people more than a couple hundred miles from their home and ask them where they're from, they'll give you the name of the signature city of their region — Chicago, St. Louis, San Francisco, Boston, wherever. Even if it's a center city they hold in contempt back home, they name it. Maybe it's just convenience, but it's also a subconscious way of saying their whole region is very important.

Political leaders recognize the region by their councils of governments and other metropolitan coordinating mechanisms. But they rarely talk the language of regionalism in public, fearing retribution at the ballot box. The contrast with business could hardly be more startling. With real markets to confront, business executives typically get the "regional" message right away. Their market for a workforce is regional. If they sell locally, "local" is regional. If they're in the international game, it's the regional platform that launches everything they do.

Environmentalists, who often ignored regional issues in their single-minded focus on such issues as air and water quality, or toxic wastes, have in recent years begun to embrace the sprawl issue, with its focus on the shared land use issues of regions.

Builders of modern Internet connections are identifying the region too. "Geography is still vital. Most of our interactions are with people in a 20- to 50-mile radius," says Seth Fearey of Collaborative Economics and lead figure in the Smart Valley collaborative effort in Silicon Valley to apply advanced information technology to solve regional problems. Cities, Fearey noted, are too small to suffice as full-purpose electronic platforms. States are too large, too distant from the focus of local needs. Regions or citistates are the right size.

... and the citizens leagues

Created afresh in the 1990s, or reborn with widened charters, citizens leagues have become leading exponents of regionalism in multiple communities across the United States. The Citizens League of Greater Cleveland, born in 1896, has twice in recent years issued its "Rating the Region" reports, showing how well or poorly the Cleveland region stacks up against comparable U.S. citistate regions on indicators from economic diversity to traffic congestion to health care costs.

A low-voltage Citizens Forum created in the 1980s for Charlotte and surrounding Mecklenburg County has been expanded dramatically to 14 counties in both North and South Carolina. The new name: Central Carolinas Choices. The territory is so large that computer linkages are being used to keep members in touch. CIRCL — the new Central Indiana Regional Citizens League formed November 1996 — represents a public admission that the single-county "Unigov" created in 1969 is geographically obsolete. Other new leagues have recently emerged in such cities as Cincinnati, Oklahoma City and Mobile.

"Citizens are hungry for a place to have a regional conversation," says William Dodge, author of the recent book, *Regional Excellence*. Citizens leagues, Dodge notes, fill the gap and let people talk about solutions that encompass entire citistate areas.

Regional consciousness

Are metropolitan areas different in their recognition of region as a vital place? The answer is clearly yes. But the precise degree of regional consciousness appears to relate, in a loose way, to the degree regional leaders have begun serious debate on the components of a healthy region — education (including workforce preparedness), the problems posed by sprawl and unwise land uses that drive up regional costs for everyone, the disparity between poor and rich, and the importance laid on the health of the downtown for the whole citistate.

Leaders in such regions as Cleveland and Atlanta seem to "have arrived" there. Portland, especially by virtue of its city conservation and land use debates, reached the regional understanding much earlier. Chattanooga is making a strong catch-up effort, though its initial civic efforts focused overwhelmingly on the city alone. Kansas City and Detroit lag in part because of the relative lack of understanding — at least until recently — that there is intimate interconnection between the quality of the workforces, their use of land, the areas' poverty problems and the center cities' fate.

Neighborhoods

Neighborhoods and community are almost synonymous in many people's minds. So is the traditional American neighborhood image — places with a mix of types of homes, sidewalks, shade trees, parks, closeby stores. Places to come from and belong to. Even after a half century of relentless construction of often bleak and standardized subdivisions, the old image sticks. The popularity of the New Urbanist or neotraditional architecture movement of the 1990s indicates a desire to return to towns — urban, suburban or indeed rural — which have accessible, friendly centers and neighborhoods of more pedestrian character and individual distinctiveness.

Neighborhoods also need to be organized to come to the table and be effective in partnerships involving their larger cities and regions. Sister Consuelo Tovar of Project Quest in San Antonio, argues: "People need to be at the table. They need to have power." Project Quest formed a partnership of the city, the community colleges and the neighborhoods. But "for it to happen," she argues, neighborhoods "had to be organized, with the credibility of having accomplished something." Leadership, in short, "wins a place at the table. Unless a community is organized, it will always be left out."

Neighborhoods relating to regions

Neighborhoods rarely have found a need or a way to connect with regional agendas. Yet the neighborhood-region connection is becoming ever-more-important, argue four Southern California academics (Manuel Pastor, Eugene Grigsby, Peter Dreier and Marta Lopez-Garza) in a 1997 report, *Growing Together*. With Hayes Foundation funding, the team examined the Los Angeles economy and the painfully slow progress of many low-income minorities since the bruising 1992 riots. Then, for comparison, it did an economic study of 73 other regions.

Sister Consuelo Tovar of Project Quest in San Antonio, argues: "People need to be at the table. They need to have power."

The conclusion: Across the U.S., reductions in center city poverty lead to more rapid income increases spread across the whole region. It's smart business for regional business and political leaders to try to deal with poor people and neighborhoods, through job training and connections, into emerging economic projects. "Doing good and doing well go hand in hand."

Two other points of common neighborhood-regional interest are emerging. One is a growing understanding that sprawl can destroy regions' environment and social order. A second is the welfare reform legislation passed in 1996. Its work requirement makes a regional approach to job location and placement critically important.

Downtowns

Finally, every region needs a heart — a downtown that works, a living room for everybody, a shared space where people of differing backgrounds can rub shoulders, a cultural and a sports mecca, a place people can take pride in.

The revival stories of such cities as Chattanooga, Cleveland, Denver, San Antonio, and San Diego would not exist if civic forces had not treasured the center cities and brought them back to life.

Portland's ultimate example

Portland may provide the ultimate example. Today the city is known for its lively downtown, graced with parks and charming street arts — and intensive activity. The McCall Waterfront Park on the Willamette River, with its winding paths and fishing piers, stands on the spot where a high-speed waterfront roadway had, as in too many cities, placed a roaring concrete artery between the city and its best natural resource, the river. Portland created a regional light rail line and created a transit mall and light rail loop in center city. It has a downtown waterfall fountain that the *New York Times'* Ada Louise Huxtable described as "one of the most important urban spaces since the Renaissance."

Much of this is attributed to Portland's Downtown Plan, implemented starting in 1972 under the reform mayor of the era, Neil Goldschmidt. The idea was to wed a successful downtown with protected neighborhoods,

The hard truth—just as it is for playing sports, repositioning a business for international competition, or sustaining a good marriage—is that everyone who cares about keeping success alive has to pay attention to the fundamentals, today and tomorrow.

advancing public transit rather than superhighways. It worked superbly.

In 1971, a prominent downtown Portland department store proposed a 12-story downtown parking garage, only to stimulate a roar of public protest.

Why? Place. The site had been purchased in 1849 by shoemaker Elijah Hill for $24 and a pair of boots. In 1858, it became site of the first public school in Oregon. In 1891, the Portland Hotel, a $1 million Victorian extravagance, opened on the site. For 60 years, its verandas, ballrooms and restaurants would be the center of Portland's downtown life.

But in 1951, the grand old hotel was razed and replaced by a two-story parking garage. That alone generated public outrage. The 12-story parking skyscraper proposal was the final straw. By broad public demand, the idea of a comprehensive Downtown Plan took shape. A number of vocal citizens, including concerned architects and neighborhood activists, expressed alarm about business interests' dominant role in the process. A highly collaborative process, balancing business, neighborhood and architectural interests, went forward.

Indeed, the Downtown Plan decreed that the parking lot site would become Portland's "central space." It took 12 more years for the ultimate solution, a grand public space known as Pioneer Courthouse Square, to emerge. Their concern for a single public space had proven critical to the remaking of their entire city. Place does matter. A great deal.

Lesson 10: *It's never over.*

Ironically, it is often the afterglow of stunning success that poses the most dangerous threat. People want to believe, "We've done it. From this point, someone else will do the work."

That's not far from what happened in Los Angeles after the 1984 Olympics. The region of gridlock had unlocked to pull off successful games. There was talk that the Olympics' masterminding director, Peter Ueberroth, might ride the triumph into the U.S. Senate, perhaps even the White House. But the Los Angeles region, sadly, frittered away the goodwill of the Olympics, failing to invest in socially troubled spots like South Central, tolerating widening divisions by race, income, and geography. It reaped a bitter harvest with the riots of 1992, besmirching the area's reputation and scaring away investors. Indeed, L.A. even failed to get an empowerment zone under federal legislation prompted by its own riots.

Keeping an eye on the fundamentals

The hard truth — just as it is for playing sports, repositioning a business for international competition, or sustaining a good marriage — is that everyone who cares about keeping success alive has to pay attention to the fundamentals, today and tomorrow.

Will Atlanta successfully face its next challenge? Can it sustain the civic energy, the outreach, the vision of its successful Olympic experience to focus on its deep social fissures, its pockets of deep poverty, and the region's endless consumption of the forest and field? Some say St. Louis peaked in 1904, Cleveland in 1950. Will future histories suggest Atlanta peaked in 1996?

Serial stories

Every successful place is a serial story, not a one-time splash. Denver is graduating from airports, convention centers, and libraries, to the tougher stuff of region-wide transportation strategies, and preserving air clean enough to see the mountains.

Charlotte's made the big map. It's a major league place now. But sustaining its quality of life will be more difficult than banks acquiring more banks.

Kansas City, while less hard-pressed than many more industrial older cities, still has to find a formula for expanding the civic club, enhancing neighborhoods, reclaiming a barren downtown, and curbing destructive sprawl.

San Diego's latest stroke of good luck is having its principal university engage the issues of the local economy and the region's binational positioning. But will there truly be the civic will to make the connections, reach tough 21st century decisions, in this sunny, relaxing place?

Denver's Downtown 16th Street Transit and Pedestrian Mall
Photo Credit: Denver Metro Chamber of Commerce

Cleveland's ongoing saga

Cleveland is moving from its miraculous-enough downtown reconstruction (who a generation ago would ever have dreamed of a Rock and Roll Hall of Fame on the lake?) to such daunting tasks as fixing one of America's most dysfunctional school systems and rebuilding confidence in neighborhoods long ravaged by poverty and disinvestment. Visit Cleveland today, get past the planning for yet another stadium (football), and it's the social agenda you hear business leaders and the mayor and foundation heads talking about.

What's encouraging is to see Mayor Mike White out in the neighborhoods, raising expectations and pushing up confidence. When Cleveland celebrated its centennial a couple of years back, there were banners hanging from the street lamp posts of struggling neighborhoods, such as Hough and Fairfax. They were commemorating a commitment — telling the world they were bringing the neighborhood back. Drive down these streets today and you see the real evidence of reinvestment — roof repairs, windows replaced, new paint, and lawns better kept. Here, one senses, is the start of a transformation, to a remade, multi-income society, that might one day remake all American cities.

Portland's ongoing challenges

Portland, Oregon, in the early 1980s, seemed to have done it all. A conservationist, neighborhood-oriented community consensus had been reached on issues ranging from nurturing the downtown and open lands protection to favoring public transportation over more expressway building. Virtually no other American community made Portland's commitments; few have enjoyed the resulting array of achievements, from conservation to downtown vitality.

Yet Portland's success is now its very problem. California expatriates, computer chip manufacturers and others have rushed in to claim a piece of the quality of life other places failed to achieve. Growth is squeezing, indeed threatening Portland's successes. The community ramped up another major civic process — 2040 — to provide the citizenry with real growth choices and renew the region's consensus over values. But the politics of conservation are getting tougher and tougher. On the one hand, there's the challenge of achieving enough added density to resist major inroads on the urban growth boundary. On the other, there are right-wing forces out to destroy the entire Metro governance plan. You won't find any civic activists in the Portland area who think the work's done.

Chattanooga rules

Ditto for Chattanooga. That first project of Chattanooga Venture, back in the 1980s, found 1,700 people participating, and produced 40 goals to be realized by the year 2000. By 1992, 37 of the goals were on their way to realization. Time to quit? No, time to start over. In 1993, when Chattanooga Venture started ReVision 2000, 2,600 people signed up, producing 2,559 recorded ideas for further improvement, boiling down to 27 new goals and 122 recommendations for actions. Now, Chattanooga has set up an Institute for Sustainability — aiming at every strategy it takes to be a completely sustaining economy and society.

After listening to a range of Chattanoogans talk about their approach, our colleague in this project, John Parr, compiled a list from their own words. The list might (though the Chattanoogans don't) be called "The Chatta-

*If there's a best practice out there, the Chattanoogans seem to find it, take it to their civic lab, and figure out whether to admire it, adopt it, or take it to another level still. And they **stick** with their agenda— a lesson that philanthropies, community and corporate, would do well to note and take to heart.*

nooga Process." We'd endorse it for any American community.

1. *Any idea is worth exploring. At the beginning, all possibilities get a respectful hearing.*

2. *Success will occur if we all sit down and put our heads together; that way, we can reach a common agenda.*

3. *There must always be a specific, but open-ended, agenda for public participation.*

4. *The collective good is always the goal, and that means the good of all citizens.*

5. *Preventing future problems and creating systemic change are always priorities in the process.*

6. *We always bring the best people in the country here to speak, advise and participate.*

7. *When necessary, we visit other communities that have been successful to find out the nuances of how and why a solution worked there, and what to avoid.*

If there's a best practice out there, the Chattanoogans seem to find it, take it to their civic lab, and figure out whether to admire it, adopt it, or take it to another level still. And they **stick** with their agenda — a lesson that philanthropies, community and corporate, would do well to note and take to heart.

A note on the future

From the vantage point of the late 1990s, the leadership challenges to America's regions seem myriad — and urgent.

Cultural and racial diversity advances dramatically, year by year, as an historically white Anglo-Saxon culture loses its majorities. This will bring dramatic change to the decision-making process, from government councils to corporate board rooms — indeed to every institution of our society.

Globalization is driving deep and growing differences of

income between the skilled and unskilled, tearing at our social fabric. Fast-advancing technology poses an array of opportunities and perils. Faceless, sprawling physical development devours land, endangers our air and water, and threatens the very character of our communities. Socially dysfunctional families and poor education throw an ominous cloud over the preparedness of our workforces, the key to our future in fierce global competition. Splintered governments make coherent regional governance immensely difficult.

Yet we found that civic entrepreneurs *are* struggling imaginatively with these challenges, starting to forge solutions in regions across the nation.

Are the citistate regions we've focused on in this paper, or the hundreds of others in America, fully prepared for the 21st century's challenges? The answer is clearly *no*. But those which *remember* that the struggle is never over, which make alertness, fresh thinking, and constant readaptation their normal mode of operating, will have the best run at the globalized age. Indeed, with their sense of adventure and experimentation, precisely those cities and regions are likely to be the most stimulating communities of the times. The kind of place one would *choose* to live.

Afterword by Project Directors Bruce Adams and John Parr

A Tool for Community Builders

Neal Peirce and Curtis Johnson have vividly described the complex leadership challenges that face community leaders as we enter the 21st century. One conclusion from our work is abundantly clear — success requires strategies that are more complex, more connected, and broader than ever before. The old way of five white guys deciding for a community is out. The new way is still evolving.

In every community we examined, we found notable achievements. And in every community we found obvious leadership gaps. As Neal and Curtis concluded: "There is no magical structure — just people and relationships." The challenge for community builders is to break through the barriers that divide and diminish our communities and help people understand they will only achieve their goals by collaborating with others.

Relationship building across traditional barriers is by definition an unnatural act. It has to be learned. It requires constant, hard work. To help, we have created a tool for community builders, a checklist for relationship building and collaborative problem solving. On one axis are the arenas in which decisions are made and actions taken that can affect communities — neighborhood, local, regional, state, national, and global. On the other axis are the players — individuals, nonprofit organizations, educational institutions, philanthropic organizations, business, and government. Players need to create partnerships among themselves and also influence decisions in as many arenas as possible.

As your community faces a problem or opportunity, the first step we recommend is to consider how each of the arenas and players might intersect. We didn't find any community that had positive interaction in every box, but we did find that healthy communities are successful because they have developed the habits of participation, communication, and collaboration.

Relationship building across traditional boundaries is by definition an unnatural act. It has to be learned. It requires constant, hard work. To help, we have created a tool for community builders, a checklist for relationship building and collaborative problem solving.

Maximizing Civic Capacity
in a Time of Increasing Complexity

ARENAS

	Neighborhood	Local	Regional	State	National	Global
Individuals						
Nonprofit Organizations						
Educational Institutions						
Philanthropic Organizations						
Business						
Government						

PLAYERS

Every community issue, whether problem or opportunity, contains the possibility for constructive action in each arena with a role for every player.

All of the players have access to and may influence, directly or indirectly, actions within each of these arenas.

Successful communities leave no opportunity to enhance and leverage their efforts uninvestigated and no partner that shares the common vision or goal uninvolved.

Everyone readily admits that issues are getting more complex. Community builders need to draw from the recent work of our counterparts in the physical sciences on "complexity" and "chaos." Simply stated: very complex systems (certainly the way any community in the United States can be described today) constantly undergo spontaneous self-organization. These complex self-organizing systems are adaptive and try to turn whatever happens to their advantage. While this adaptive process is very dynamic, it does not have to lead to weirdly unpredictable gyrations known as chaos. An effectively operating complex system comes into balance at the edge of chaos. The key to operating effectively at the edge of chaos is the ability to see potential connections and act on them.

Success occurs in communities where there is communication, coordination and collaborative action by many entities, institutions, organizations, agencies and individuals. On specific issues, successful communities have the ability to see the connections and act on them.

This is where our checklist comes into play — to help you develop this instinct for collaboration. This tool will help community builders think beyond their immediate responsibilities and help you focus on larger, longer term possibilities. The future of community leadership in the next century depends upon our capacity to develop what John Gardner calls "networks of responsibility," people crossing boundaries and learning how to work together. We hope this checklist is a tool that helps your community make the transformation.

a Reading List

The case studies that serve as the foundation for this report have been published as a companion volume, *Boundary Crossers: Case Studies of How Ten of America's Metropolitan Regions Work*. Copies of the case studies are available on The Academy of Leadership's CivicSource web page at http://civicsource.org or by sending $15 to: CivicSource, The Academy of Leadership, The University of Maryland, College Park, MD 20742-7715. We recommend these case studies to those of you who want to dig more deeply into the stories behind this report.

As we did our work, we came across others struggling with these same critical issues of community building. We recommend to you some of our favorite recent books on this subject:

Harry Boyte and Nancy Kari, *Building America: The Democratic Promise of Public Work* (Philadelphia: Temple University Press, 1996).

David Chrislip and Carl E. Larson, *Collaborative Leadership: How Citizens & Civic Leaders Can Make a Difference* (San Francisco: Jossey-Bass, 1994).

Henry Cisneros, *Interwoven Destinies: Cities and the Nation* (New York: Norton, 1993).

William R. Dodge, *Regional Excellence: Governing Together to Compete Globally and Flourish Locally* (Washington: National League of Cities, 1996).

John W. Gardner, *On Leadership* (New York: The Free Press, 1990).

Ronald Heifetz, *Leadership Without Easy Answers* (Cambridge: Harvard University Press, 1994).

Douglas Henton, John Melville and Kimberly Walesh, *Grassroots Leaders for a New Economy: How Civic Entrepreneurs Are Building Prosperous Communities* (San Francisco: Jossey-Bass, 1997).

Daniel Kemmis, *The Good City and the Good Life: Renewing the Sense of Community* (New York: Houghton Mifflin, 1995).

John Kretzmann and John McKnight, *Building Community from the Inside Out* (Evanston: Center for Urban Affairs and Policy Research, Northwestern University, 1993).

Frances Moore Lappé and Paul Martin DuBois, *The Quickening of America* (San Francisco: Jossey-Bass, 1994).

Larraine R. Matusak, *Finding Your Voice* (San Francisco: Jossey-Bass, 1997).

Harold A. McDougall, *Black Baltimore: A New Theory of Community* (Philadelphia: Temple University Press, 1993).

Neal R. Peirce, Curtis W. Johnson, and John Stuart Hall, *Citistates: How Urban America Can Prosper in a Competitive World* (Washington: Seven Locks Press, 1993).

Robert H. Rosen, *Leading People: Transforming Business from the Inside Out* (New York: Viking, 1996).

Lisbeth Schorr, *Common Purpose: Strengthening Families and Neighborhoods to Rebuild America* (New York: Doubleday, 1997).

William Julius Wilson, *When Work Disappears: The World of the New Urban Poor* (New York: Knopf, 1996).

These important reports will deepen your understanding of what is working in America's communities today:

The America Project, *Linked Future: Building Metropolitan Communities* (Atlanta: A Conference Held at The Carter Center, January 27-28, 1997).

The Annie E. Casey Foundation, *The Path of Most Resistance: Reflections on Lessons Learned from New Futures* (Baltimore: 1995).

Eisenhower Leadership Group, *Democracy at Risk: How Schools Can Lead* (College Park: The Academy of Leadership, 1996).

International & Public Affairs Center, Occidental College, *Growing Together: Linking Regional & Community Development in a Changing Economy* (Los Angeles: 1997).

Pew Partnership for Civic Change, *Leadership Collaboration Series* (Charlottesville: 1996).

The Rockefeller Foundation, *Stories of Renewal: Community Building and the Future of Urban America* (New York: 1997).

Together We Can, *Building Community: Exploring New Relationships Across Service Systems Reform, Community Organizing, and Community Economic Development* (Washington: Institute for Educational Leadership, 1997).

During the course of our work we came across several websites that readers may find useful:

Brookings Institution Center on Urban and Metropolitan Policy — www.brookings.edu/es/urbancen

Center for Neighborhood Technology — www.cnt.org

Citistates Group — www.citistates.com

Civic Practices Network — www.cpn.org

National Civic League — www.ncl.org

and a Word of Thanks

We have been given a gift, the gift of reflection. For each of us, the 1980s and the early-90s were a whirlwind of activity. Bruce served eight years as an elected county councilmember in Montgomery County, Maryland. John served as president of the National Civic League for a decade. As co-project directors of the effort that produced this report, we are grateful for the opportunity to dig deeply into the civic DNA of these ten metropolitan areas of the country. It has been a wonderful and enriching exercise.

Just over twenty-five years ago, we each had the great good fortune to meet John Gardner. He was building the national citizens organization Common Cause, and we were young recruits in his army of citizens. John Gardner has been a dear friend and great mentor to both of us. In January of 1996, we took a group of solid thinkers and reflective activists to visit with him at Stanford University. There this project was born. The meeting, sponsored by the Kellogg Leadership Studies Project, was co-chaired by John Gardner and Georgia Sorenson, and attended by James MacGregor Burns, The Academy of Leadership; Cheryl Casciani, Citizens Planning and Housing Association (Baltimore); Henry Izumizaki, Oakland Urban Strategies Council; Kathryn Johnson, The Healthcare Forum; Beth Kellar, International City-County Management Association; Dan Kemmis, Mayor of Missoula, Montana; Harold McDougall, Catholic University; John McKnight, Northwestern University; Bruce Miroff, SUNY Albany; Carl Moore, Western Network; Kathy Novak, Northglenn (Colorado) City Councilwoman representing the National League of Cities; Gayle Oberst, Gulf Coast Community College; Laura Pinkney, San Francisco Mayor's Office of Children, Youth, & Families; Jan Purdy, Citizens League of Greater Cleveland; and Rosemary Romero, Western Network.

With initial support from the Ewing Marion Kauffman Foundation, we recruited a first rate project team led by John Gardner and including Curtis Johnson, chairman of the Metropolitan Council of the Twin Cities and former chief of staff to the Governor of Minnesota; Harold McDougall, professor of law at Catholic Univer-

69

sity and author of *Black Baltimore: A New Theory of Community;* Suzanne Morse, executive director of the Pew Partnership for Civic Change and former director of programs at the Kettering Foundation; Neal Peirce, the country's premier columnist on regional, state, and neighborhood affairs and lead author of *Citistates;* Robert Rosen, founder of the Healthy Companies Institute and author of *Leading People: Transforming Business from the Inside Out;* and Annette Rogers, a doctoral student in sociology at the University of Maryland who served as our project assistant.

San Diego, California Skyline
Photo Credit: Joanne DiBona/San Diego Convention & Visitors Bureau

The Center for the Study of Community hosted the first meeting of the project team on July 19 & 20, 1996 in Santa Fe, New Mexico at Sol y Sombra. Our special thanks to our gracious hosts Beth and Charles Miller and Cheryl Charles for providing a magnificent setting and important insights for the start of our work. Robin Gerber, The Academy of Leadership; Michael Kinsley, Rocky Mountain Institute; Carl Moore, Western Network; Robert Sherman, Surdna Foundation; and Georgia Sorenson, The Academy of Leadership, joined in the discussions. We established the ground rules for the project and selected three cities to begin our research—Charlotte, Kansas City, and Portland, Oregon. After completing the field research for these cities, the project team met in Washington, DC on October 18, 1996 to hear a presentation from Marc Weiss of the U.S. Department of Housing and Urban Development, refine the project

goals, and select the other seven cities —Atlanta, Chatta-
nooga, Cleveland, Denver, Detroit, San Antonio, and San
Diego. With support from CivicSource, a W.K. Kellogg
Foundation funded project at The James MacGregor
Burns Academy of Leadership at The University of
Maryland headed by former Houston Mayor Kathryn
Whitmire, we completed the field research and wrote
initial drafts of the case studies.

On April 25 & 26, 1997, with support from the Kauffman
Foundation and the hospitality of Thomas Lovejoy and
Sarah Boren of The Smithsonian Institution, the project
team held our final meeting in the Woodrow Wilson
Library of The Smithsonian Castle. Representatives of
the ten case study cities commented on the case study
drafts and participated in discussions of lessons learned:
Mike Burton, elected executive officer of Metro,
Portland's regional government; Ann Coulter, executive
director of the Chattanooga Hamilton County Regional
Planning Agency; Shirley Franklin, former chief admin-
istrative officer of the City of Atlanta and former chief
operating officer of the Atlanta Committee for the
Olympic Games; Allegra (Happy) Haynes, Denver City
Councilwoman; James Nunnley, anti-drug program
administrator of Jackson County, Missouri (Kansas City);
Jan Purdy, executive director of the Citizens League of
Greater Cleveland; Gloria Robinson, director of planning
and development of the City of Detroit; William
Seelbach, chair of Inverness Casting Group and founder
and first president of Cleveland Tomorrow; Francis
Brackett Thompson, senior program manager, The
Lynnwood Foundation (Charlotte); Sister Consuelo
Tovar, lead organizer, San Antonio COPS; and Mary
Walshok, associate vice chancellor, University of Califor-
nia, San Diego.

In addition, our April conference at the Smithsonian was
enriched by the participation of: Cheryl Charles, Center
for the Study of Community; Richard Couto, Jepson
School of the University of Richmond; Phyllis Jeffers,
The Academy of Leadership; Bruce Katz, The Brookings
Institution; Beth Kellar, International City-County
Management Association; M. Faith Mitchell, National
Academy of Sciences; Farley Peters, Citistates Group;
Georgia Sorenson, The Academy of Leadership; Ellen
Schall, New York University; Mary Walsh, National

League of Cities; Ron Walters, The Academy of Leadership; and Marc Weiss, U.S. Department of Housing and Urban Development.

This was one of those wonderful projects where many people gave far more of themselves than we had any right to expect. Our very special thanks to: Leon Eplan, the former commissioner of planning and development for the City of Atlanta; Jan Purdy, executive director of the Citizens League of Greater Cleveland; Betty Chafin Rash of Central Carolinas Choices; and Mary Walshok of the University of California, San Diego. Thanks also to Ann Lang and David Sanders in Detroit; Gerri Spring and Eleanor Cooper in Chattanooga; Cindy Sefler Ballard and Brent Schondelmeyer in Kansas City. And to Barbara Shapiro whose editorial skills made our case studies much more enjoyable to read; to Annette Rogers, our project assistant, who labored mightily to get the demographic information on the cities for our case studies and the photographs for this report as well as organizing the Smithsonian conference; to Matt Eisenberg for solving computer glitches large and small; and to Tony Franquelli and Carla Conway of University of Maryland Printing Services. Last but most certainly not least, many thanks to our wives—Peggy Engel and Sandy Widener—who not only put up with our travel and late nights but then were called on once again for their superior writing and editing talents. This report is stronger because of their efforts well beyond the call of duty.

Bruce Adams
Senior Fellow
The Academy of Leadership
The University of Maryland
College Park, Maryland

John Parr
Principal
Center for Regional & Neighborhood Action
Denver, Colorado

October 1997